Amir A

Triumphs and Tribulations of a Trainee Solicitor

An Inside Story

To my mother

All my successes are down to you

Contents

These pages here are equivalent of diary notes, streams of consciousness, and raging rants, desperately attempting to articulate my experiences that have culminated in me qualifying as a solicitor of the Senior Courts of England and Wales. Names, dates and places have been changed. Nothing mentioned here is intended to persuade or dissuade you from the legal profession. I am protecting my identity by utilising the alias of 'Amir A'.

1. Get Moving

July 2014

The compulsory Legal Practice Course completed. Massive law loan debt accrued. Now it's time to roll up my sleeves and get my size 8s through the door of a law firm – any law firm. Ten applications sent a day. Website after website after website of legal recruitment. Walked into several recruitment agencies. CV in hand, heart on sleeve. Surely, someone will accidentally misread my CV and hire me. Months pass and not even a squeak.

Time to tighten the belt and opt for even less. Minimum wage admin role at firm? That's asking for too much. Internship must be the only way in. Maybe I can start somewhere and work my way up? Start microbial and aggressively rise into a pandemic.

Again, 10 applications sent a day. A further two months elapses. Still no reply. Finally, after months of sending chaser after chaser, calling up the firm's HR department five minutes after my CV and cover letter hit their inbox, a law firm replied. An entire law firm with actual solicitors working there agreed to see me. I even stalked their profiles on Law Society (official website listing solicitors and firms). They seemed real.

October 2014

I was told to report to the reception of this law firm and someone will come and pick me up. I wore my best, and at that point, only suit. A depressing grey tailored for a middle-aged man, straight off the rack. Loose in all the wrong places. A suit I wore at my brother's wedding, my graduation and now my first proper law interview. I woke up early and could not eat anything. Nerves were getting to me. I decide to get there early. That's what those cookie-cutter interview-advice websites say. The weather is warm as London basks in a summer that year that overran into autumn for a little too long. I board one of London's finest red buses as it rattles and shakes to the stop I need to get off at. The moment I step foot outside the bus, Google Maps on my phone confirms that I have "arrived at my destination". It sounded poetic. My whole life has brought me to this point. Google Maps has become a metaphor for the divine map of my legal career. "You have arrived at your destination". Right here, right now. I was thinking about bargaining for a full-time position straight away. Maybe even hustle for a neat salary, a gym membership and maybe a season loan discount on my travel. I have seen the legal adverts online. I have watched the movies. It is high time. I walk up to the building which unfortunately was in an industrial estate, which to be completely honest, did not fill me with any excitement. I brushed it aside though. The firm had a bullish name: Black Tiger Law. Wow. The main partner has been cited in some legal column of a tabloid newspaper. Double wow. Their website says they work on a "business to business" strategy which made them the "right choice for you". For me, definitely.

I step inside, sweat spreading across my brow and at my pits. I talk to a receptionist at the front desk. "Which company have you come to see?", she says drily. "Black Tiger Law", I sputter. I realise the building is not theirs – rather they rent a space in the building, like numerous other companies and institutions. Nevertheless, I am eager. These minor ego defeats will not dwindle my determination. I sit down waiting for someone to "pick me up". I wait. 9am is my interview. It's now 9:50am. They must be busy. It's normal. They're a law firm probably working on a groundbreaking case.

Finally, a small diminutive lady hurries to me and tells me to follow her. She sits me down in a random corner of the building, looking over the car park situated near the back of the building. The paint on the walls were peeling around me. She points at a rusting metal chair near the fire exit door, to which I quickly sit on. She explains that they have looked at my CV and are impressed. Her eyes looked down joyously at the writing I put on that piece of paper. Looking back at it now, I had a run of the mill law degree from a mediocre law school. I had no particular legal experience, and my expertise extended to a handful of telephone complaints handler (call centre zombie employee), court administration officer (court runner, which entails running between courts updating a list of cases scribbled on the court doors), and child support officer (a spare hand in a day care when I was 13 years old).

She breaks the moment with what I was not exactly expecting, since she pre-empted the entire conversation with "CV" and "impressed".

"This role is initially unpaid for at least a period of three to six months. And then if we are impressed, we'll offer you a full time role in no time."

I was expecting two weeks, maybe a month. But three to six months! Surely the salary must be sweet later, since I would have already done enough manual labour to pay for what I assume to be the partner's latest Audi Q8 parked infront of the window next to a wall sign of 'Black Tiger Law'.

"Yes", she replies excitedly.

"You're set for at least a salary of 12 thousand maybe even rising to 13 thousand a year depending on performance."

Three years at law school. One year completing the mammoth legal practice course that set me back 13,800GBP already. Tens of applications a day. All for one opportunity at Black Tiger Law for a possible 12 to 13 thousand, after six months of what can only be described as indebted servitude. Sign me up!

I tell her that I have to hand in my notice to my current employer (imaginary), and I'll be there as soon as I can.

November 2014

I start my first day at my first legal job. I wake up bright and early as Britain returns to its default weather of wet, grey and windy, and head to the office. I still feel slightly let down by the meagre possible salary and the need to complete an unpaid trial period, but it didn't faze me enough to stop me. They tell me to get there at 9am. I am there at 8:45am. Impressive. I inform the receptionist of my presence, I sit down, and I wait. 45 minutes elapse. No sight of anyone actually taking me to Black Tiger Law's whopper of an office with its award-winning, journal-cited, young, bright, and groundbreaking partner. I start to worry. Did they change their mind and I just haven't been informed? Did I read the correct start date? I walk up to the receptionist and she gestures to me to sit back down.

"They know you're here. I told them three times already," she croaks after an awkward silence.

Finally, a young man with an old face turns up and takes me to the office. I ask him about the woman that interviewed me. He says she is no longer with us. I'm not sure if he means she died or just moved on to another job.

The entire office was in a small corner of the building. Not more than 15 metres by 15. At least thirty young-looking people are huddled around one desk, headsets on, whispering down the phone. He points me to my chair and gives me a worn out manual.

"Read it and get started. Ask anyone if you need help." I sat there reading intently.

"Turn on your head set. Speak clearly. Record invoices properly on the system. Make sure you push for the highest price possible". This did not sound legalese. This sounded and looked suspiciously like the 6.80GBP an hour call centre job down the road that I rinsed out during my university days. I ask my brand new colleague hunched next to me where the award-winning, journal-cited, young, bright, and groundbreaking partner is (not in those exact words). She shrugs and continues typing away at her PC.

Three hours in, and many manuals read and forgotten, a goblin-sized creature strolls in with a pack of Sainsbury's coleslaw. She gives me a funny look as she walks by me, as if I am a squatter that has decided to live on her porch. She sits there eating her coleslaw as she picks up a headset, and starts barking orders down the phone.

"If you were injured at work we can help you! PPI? We can do that. You don't know what that is? Where have you been living?!" She says to what I assume is an old lady on the other end she probably cold-called and/or bought her number from a telephone database.

I ask the man that brought me if I can help him with anything to get a feel of things. He points at his headset signalling to leave him alone. I ask the melting woman on my other side if lunch is soon. She intently ignores. I look around this small space with many human-shaped zombies hunched over PCs and no one accidentally gives me eye contact. I stand up and whisper to the table that I am going to the bathroom. Not a flicker of conscience. I put on my grey blazer and make my way out of the building. I do not even look back. What do I tell my mum if she asks why I am back early? Embarrassing. My ego? Shattered.

December 2014

My ten applications a day routine has swelled to 30 applications a day after my nightmare start. My once singular CV has morphed into numerous tailored CVs, each peppered with a different legal spice to appeal to different law firms. Turns out, law firms come in numerous shapes and sizes. Some are high street firms, mainly focused on wills and probate, immigration, family and crime. These are usually funded by way of Legal Aid, where the firm reaches out to the Legal Aid Agency, cap in hand, all but begging for some money because they helped a poor soul with his case by sending a few emails, sitting in his police interview, and telling him how much of a tough position he is in (funnily enough, this is the sort of place I end up doing my legal training contract at).

Larger firms, the ones in shiny buildings somewhere in the City of London, require a more nuanced approach. They want your CV and a well-written cover letter explaining why you're a perfect hand-in-glove fit for the job. They also want you to bin it and to go on their specifically designed website and upload it in a certain fashion on their specially made portal. That portal leads you down to their state-of-the-art AI-controlled application page where they take every detail of yours down to the grade you got in your first exam back in year 2. Then they request a copy of your transcripts and certificates. A referee would do, too. Actually, make it three referees: a professional, academic and personal referee, all vouching to your unshakeable character and legal knowledge. Experiences? They want all of them. Part-time judge at The Hague, youngest violinist in your continent, 5 years experience at the other carbon copy firm in the shiny building opposite, and know-how of the job down to minutiae of when the tea breaks are (trick question, there aren't any). How about a few paragraphs about how they are different to all the other places in all the other shiny buildings?

"Why do you like to practise *INSERT TYPE OF LAW THAT YOU NEVER HEARD OF TWO YEARS AGO* here with us rather than with our identical twin down the road?"

You know it's the money and status, but you can't say that. They want you to whisper sweet nothings in their electronic portal AI-controlled state-of-the-art ears. Once this is done, you have to complete a series of online tests. The numerical reasoning, situational judgment and critical thinking tests. To make things more interesting, you are no longer trying to hit a specific pass mark, rather beat a certain percentage of the other candidates who you do not know and will most likely never see.

Once you triumph in the dark against all odds, you are invited to an assessment centre. There the circus starts again with some mundane teamwork activities and presentations, interviews with the old men and women of the HR department, spear throwing, sit ups, bench press, fire-breathing and a game of Chess against Deep Blue. Then you are rejected in a swift copy-and-paste email sent to 99% of applicants the next working day and you are reminded that the next "opening for potential trainees" is "only" nine months down the line. Efficient. Precise. Effective.

Three applications a year of this type will have you contemplating throwing in the towel – believe me.

Side note: acquaintances that have successfully managed to pass through this process at the shiny buildings do indeed end up on a very bulky salary… that are largely spent on the coffee machines, canteens and the purchasing of new underwear in the aforementioned shiny building. They devote their lives to the financial well-being companies and other entities without a pat on the back or thank you. Is it worth it? That is down to your interpretation.

2. The Wilderness Years

January 2015 to January 2017

I accidentally fell into work at a small non-government organisation that simply wanted a person that is willing to learn on the job, can write in clear English and a Middle Eastern language, send some emails, make some phone calls and be a bit nice to everyone. I enjoyed my time at this place thoroughly. The pay was anemic no doubt, the job was uncertain for sure, but I was finally sinking my teeth into a legitimate place of employment. The hours were good, too. You generally come in on time and leave on time.

I worked on interesting projects including advocating for a death penalty moratorium in various countries, attending the UN Human Rights Council in Geneva, and networking with larger NGOs on similar projects. It felt moral and ethical at every turn, and made me feel like my work was always worthwhile. No doubt, it helped me grow as a human and I am forever indebted to the employer at that time that allowed me to grow and foster awareness of the challenges facing various people across the world.

However, I still felt a yearning to put my now slowly ageing law degree to some use. I reminded myself that I put in a substantial amount of time and money to become a "lawyer". Every year, new people are graduating with a law degree and further saturating the market. I come from a family that has no university graduates, let alone lawyers. I was born and bred here in the UK, surrounded by opportunities. Yes, the shiny buildings application punched the breath out of me and I deep down knew that I am not a corporate suit. I had interests in smaller, less commercial enterprises, involved in things like human rights. I was enjoying spouting these phrases in my time at the small NGO I was at. It made me and everyone around me feel human, rather than raging cogs in a machine desperate to quantify and make the most monetarily from every living creature.

Family and close friends also added some background noise.

"This job you're in is not secure."

"Make use of your law degree. Every year more law graduates are flooding the market."

"Why have you stopped applying?"

"What's next? Any plans?"

They were well intentioned. I do not begrudge them for that pressure.

After a two-year period of relative relaxation in the NGO, I decided to do what I always heard people say: it's who you know, not what you know. I asked certain members of my immediate family if they know of a place or someone that would take on a law graduate. These members spoke to their acquaintances who spoke to their acquaintances. Surprisingly someone informed my sister in-law that she applied to a place who had a pretty sweet CEO, and he's "always looking for someone".

I sent over my CV, which was passed on through a matrix of acquaintances until finally landing at this CEO's desk. Let us call him Adam. He replied to me in a polite email at 12am.

"Hi, My name is Adam and I am the CEO of Good Omen Law Ltd. I would love to see you. Anytime you're free, give me a call!"

Suspicious timing for a reply but a flicker of light in what was a long tunnel of darkness. Maybe there is hope after all.

3. Plight under the Pharaoh

February 2017

I scheduled an interview with Adam at his office. His office was situated in the heart of the City in London in a historic building. I took the London Underground there. Big Ben was not far off and was visible from his office. It was certainly an impressive building in an equally impressive location.

I had to tame my reignited ego. It does not matter where he is situated. I wanted a genuine legal role with a decent salary, with a reasonable amount of training and exposure. I did not care for the name or the location. I was wary of being played by what can only be described as legal vultures, preying on the energy and youth of young graduates.

Adam came down the lift to greet me in the lobby. He was dressed in a smart blue shirt but had his top button open. His smile was warm and eyes polite. He was exuding confidence and friendliness. There was a spring in his step. His handshake was firm and he immediately tried to establish rapport with me.

"Lovely suit! Do you want a coffee? You look like a coffee drinker." I am a heavy coffee drinker.

He took me to the lounge and personally made me a coffee. He pointed at Big Ben from the window and made some quip about the history of the building, which now I do not recall in detail. He seemed to be genuinely a nice man that wanted to impress me as much as I was aiming to impress him. Good start, Amir, but do not get carried away. Ask the right questions, and let's see what he has to say.

He sat me down in his office. The table was spotless. All files were arranged perfectly across his cabinet behind his table. Not a speck of dust on any surface. Pencils perfectly sharpened. Paperclips put in an orderly line.

"Amir, I have looked at your CV. You do not have much experience but I can see that you're passionate after reading your cover letter. Moreover, I see myself in you somewhat. I also worked at NGOs before I became a lawyer. I have a passion similar to yours and I do take on pro bono clients. I wish to hire you as a legal caseworker to kick start your career."

I was impressed by that opening.

"What about my legal training?"

He was quick to reply. "I will oversee your training personally and will send you to courses, and one day provide you with a training contract so that you may qualify as a solicitor – if you're interested."

He was playing with my heart strings, and had me at the edge of my seat.

"Don't make a decision today. Go home and think about it, because I am serious about training you myself. But first, let me show you your future colleagues."

He walked me to the entrance of the room opposite his and explained outside that this is where his solicitors and caseworkers "make the magic", with a cheeky grin. He swung the door open and five employees looked at us in fright, like a farmer entering a chicken coop. They proceeded to all say "Hi Adam" in a chorus after he looked at them. Flashbacks of Black Tiger Law seared through my mind. I pushed away that thought.

He took me back to his office, told me to finish my coffee, and inform him of my decision this week.

I left his office on a cloud of hope. I will be trained by Adam, I will have training opportunities, I can likely qualify as a solicitor at his firm, and he seems like a nice enough person to work under. I went home and thought about the opportunity the whole night. I checked online to see if there was anyone that previously worked at the firm and if they have left any feedback. Nothing. The reviews from clients were mainly five stars on various ratings websites. I thought I was being too careful and should just take the jump. Which is exactly what I did the following day. I called him up. He greeted me warmly and seemed to be smiling while he spoke, as the words flowed positively and fluidly.

"I would like to take on the opportunity to work as a legal caseworker at Good Omens, and hope I will impress you enough to be awarded with a training contract."

"Excellent, Amir. I am eagerly awaiting your start. No doubt I will provide you with all the training necessary to make you a great solicitor!"

Start date agreed, I counted down the days.

06 February 2017

I arrived at the Good Omen's building even earlier than my arrival at my interview at Black Tiger Law. The winter sun was just starting to pierce the winter morning. Adam's secretary greeted me at the lounge and she brought me up to the office. Adam was working away already. She showed me around and introduced me to the employees. The people I saw were different to the ones that greeted me on the day of my interview. Or was that my memory just acting up?

Adam then waltzed in, shoes shining bright, and showed me to my desk. He was cordial and smiled a lot. The employees all smiled with him.

He then left to continue his work. The faces of the employees changed to that of misery. It must be Monday blues, I thought.

Slowly, they began to chatter among themselves, all but bitching about Adam. I was shocked. Adam did not give me an impression that he was anything but a hardworking pleasant boss. Why are they talking negatively about him?

He stuck his head through the door and they all went dead silent. He then whispered with a mischievous smile, "Hey Amir, come to my office. Let me hand you your first case."

I walked to his spotless office. I sit down, and he hands me a large file. The file was perfectly tabbed. Not a crease on any paper and the handwriting looked like it was etched by a sentient AI.

"Take a read of my notes and read the manuals I have drafted. Then begin work on this case. This client wishes to invest substantially in the UK and needs to obtain the necessary visa for this to happen. And you know me! I make dreams happen. Best of luck and pop in if you need any help."

I return to my desk. Two colleagues noticed the file in my hands, and were craning their necks to peer at the name of the client written on it.

"He has already given you an excellent case. I have been here for 4 months and he has given me nothing but chicken feed", one of the employees blurted.

This caused a stir and their faces all went sour. He snuck his head in, appeared to be listening, and walked back to his office.

I felt Adam had a soft spot for me. He's already trusting me with casework and surely respects me enough to hand me a decent case. These colleagues are simply being bitter.

07 February 2017

One of the more vocal colleagues was called in to Adam's office. She returns upset. She picks up her things, leaves the entry key fob on her desk, and leaves.

The other colleague leans in and whispers, "She was the most senior solicitor here."

01 March 2017

An intern joins. She prints a form that is requested by Adam. The printer needs paper. She puts in a brand new batch and proceeds to print. She shows it to Adam. Adam exclaims, "Why did you not use scrap paper? Do you not care for the environment?!"

The intern returns to the printer. Adam follows. Adam exclaims, "have you never seen a printer before? Is there anything in there? And I am not talking about the printer"

Two hours pass.

The intern decides to go for lunch and returns later. Adam is at the door waiting. "I observed that your lunch break overran for 5 minutes".

The intern went to the toilet. All the employees were now intrigued with this obvious spectacle being made by Adam. I and another colleague pretended to have a need to pop to the bathroom. Adam stood outside the female toilets staring at his wristwatch. As the intern came out of the toilet, he startled her as he stepped in front of the door. "15 minutes in the toilet?"

The intern then went for a cigarette break. She was never seen again.

03 March 2017

One of my colleagues faced a volcanic Adam that lambasted her for not sending out a periodic email to a client I have never heard of. She had a track record of never taking the blame for anything that goes wrong. But who will she blame this time, I wondered? She hurries to the room and points at me to Adam.

"He is the one that was told by me to do it and he forgot." Adam looked at me sternly for a few seconds and then sprinted back to his office.

"Amir, you f******* idiot, it was your job to do this task every month, don't you remember?" she said as she sat down panting, her panicked demeanour turning to a giddiness.

No, I do not remember, since I damn well knew it wasn't my job to do anything other than to focus on the only case Adam designated me to do. However, I was new and did not want trouble. I took the blame despite not even knowing what went wrong.

Blaming others. An Olympic sport in the legal profession.

06 March 2017

I have been at Good Omen a month now. I have tried to work diligently and asked questions when needed to progress my now growing caseload. It is still early days. Adam has sort of allowed me free reign. I start to realise that his treatment of others was very different to how he was treating me. I was now beginning to feel guilty but still did not stand up for my colleagues. I realised that they were jaded and worked to the bone by Adam with no appreciation. He truly did run a tight ship.

I felt that I finalised my first case. I was now required to present it to Adam. I secretly felt that I will impress him. I worked diligently for weeks on end until 9pm everyday trying to perfect the evidence bundle, and writing excellent legal arguments utilising various key caselaw that I learnt whilst reading on the train to work. The documents that I obtained in support were running in the hundreds of pages, all neatly tabbed just like how Adam does it.

I walk in to his office and he is standing behind a new intern with his arms crossed, which he has placed next to his desk. He is commanding her to dictate his exact words in reply to a complaint he received from a client.

"Type it exactly as I say. Can you not hear me?" he exclaims to the stressed intern as I sit in front of his desk. I can see her hands shaking.

"Hi Amir. I hope you enjoyed your month. I will be with you momentarily, if that is okay with you?" he tells me calmly as his eyes remain firmly fixed on the back of the intern's head.

He proceeds to shunt the intern from the room and sits at the helm of his desk.

Adam begins a methodical examination of my case bundle. His eyes moving from page to page in a robotic fashion. He hums to himself under his breath.

"Amir, this is badly drafted. As you can see here, you pressed space twice." He takes out a red pen and circles the space where the crime happened.

"Also, your bundle is in incorrect order. I like it like this. Do you understand?" He shuffles two pieces of paper in reverse order. It made no particular sense but I nodded.

"Go back to your desk and redraft this." He scribbled a series of corrections that mainly revolved around font, size and spaces.

I go back to my desk. The intern that he scared away from the room is crying at my desk. The other colleagues are trying to console her. I too try to console her, but the rest of the colleagues stared at me angrily, as I begin to realise that they think that I am Adam's mole.

The honeymoon period is soon to be over.

20 March 2017

I am told by Adam that I have to attend with a client to a registry office to submit some documents. I wait in the lounge area. A chauffeur arrives and asks for me. I show my face. He tells me that the client is not here but has provided an assistant who will accompany me to the registry office to hand over these documents.

I get in the fancy car. We drive down to the registry office. I queue up in the building and once I get to the front of the queue and enter a booth, I hand over a letter of authority confirming my client's instructions and Adam's business card.

"What kind of name is Good Omens?" the registry officer snorts.

03 April 2017

Adam continued to trash my case bundles one after another, and would simultaneously hand me more complex cases. I knew there was going to be a learning curve but I started to wonder when it would curve up. When there were no issues with the bundles, he would comment that my desk requires tidying up, or that my latest email was not pleasant enough to the client, or that my lunch break overran by a minute.

Adam began peeking through the blinds at us as we worked. He would send out weird emails to all at the firm explaining that the cake break we took at 7pm was "unprofessional, and Good Omen is paying you all your salary – which you all should bare in my mind at all times and not indulge in frivolous activities."

On one occasion, he walked in, looked at me and immediately scurried to his desk. An email popped up in all our inboxes. "Reminder – please ensure your beards are regularly trimmed to a reasonable height."

Seeing as all my colleagues were female and I was the only male employee, he surely meant the hairy new female intern that joined yesterday.

17 April 2017

I was typing away at my computer with one hand whilst massaging my temple with the other, as I felt a headache come on. I have been battling recurrent bouts of migraines since

Adam upped the ante. Adam scurried into the room, which I did not see. Late nights and early mornings were starting to take a physical toll on me.

Two hands on the keyboard at all times, Amir!"

03 May 2017

At this point of my time at Good Omen, I had seen an entire new team replace the old team. I was the last man standing. The four months there felt like eons and my hair began to fall when I showered. This did not happen before. I was beginning to feel a burning sensation across my chest and pressure behind my eyes. Sunday nights would be filled with dread as I thought about my caseload and having to face Adam on Monday.

I had learnt to complete case after case, and every single time, Adam was not happy with the work. His comments were turning more scathing by the day. The most recent being "are you even worth the salary I pay you?"

His emails became increasingly clear.

"I expect you to be here before I am in the office and work until I leave. Coming in on weekends will also not kill you. All this is being noted and any training contract opportunities hinge on your level of dedication to me and the firm." I have never seen Adam even leave the office, so coming in before him is like asking if you can give birth to your own mother.

I began returning home and would stare in the open for prolonged periods of time. My wife, ever quick to assess my situation, begged me to quit work and promised that she would help finance our living (rent and all) whilst I searched for new work. She began sending out CVs on my behalf in desperate hope that I can find an alternative job. My wife urged me to stand up to him and not let him walk all over me.

I walk in to work on Monday and picked up my most recent case bundle to get approved by Adam. I was ready to be incinerated by his comments. I walk in to his office and he is signing an application, which I recognise as one of my former clients. I approach his desk and he has signed the application in the style of my former client's signature. He proceeds to shuffle the bundle out of sight, and in to one of his drawers it goes.

I hand him the bundle, and as he holds it, he immediately picks up a hair off the top of the bundle. "How unprofessional this is. A hair on my bundle? Disgusting."

I break character and immediately point at Adam, and in a commanding voice tell him to see me in the lounge.

I walk out and he does not follow straight away. I do not wait for him. I walk straight to the lounge, sit and wait. He walks into the lounge after a substantial amount of time.

I begin to fight my tears as I scramble to find words to explain my increasing difficulty in working at Good Omen. I try to weigh every word as I begin to articulate how he has worked me hard almost every day, usually after my contracted hours, how I am desperate to impress him, and how I have attempted to learn from my mistakes, progress and improve my cases.

He retorts, "if you were at any other firm, you would be worked until 12am. You are lucky to be working here".

I snap back at him saying, "different teams have come and left. Solicitor after solicitor, caseworker after caseworker, and intern after intern. They all left this damned place because of you. You can't hold onto anybody. You do not respect me or any employee."

My voice breaks and I feel my eyes water.

Suddenly, Adam's features change. His sour face dissolves and he begins to smile warmly – the same smile I saw in our first interview. He tells me that it's going to be okay. He leans back and the Adam of the interview day appears in full.

"I am sorry you feel this way. I am under stress too. Do you know what, Amir? Let me make you a coffee."

He proceeds to make me a coffee. He returns and manages to change the topic. He speaks about the weather, the history of the building and Big Ben outside the window.

He then stretches out his hand and states with warmth in his voice, "I am sorry you feel this way and I will try to improve. I will make you a great solicitor, Amir. Just be patient."

I hesitantly shake it. We walk back to his office and he pats me on my back and tells me to go to my desk and enjoy the rest of my day.

04 May 2017

I return to work the following day. Adam has moved my entire desk into his room. He points at me and shouts "You! You work right here in front of me from now on."

35

I begin work at my new desk, adjacent to Adam's. He watches me as I type away, face sullen and serious. Eyes fixed on me. The only sound I can hear is the whizz of the air conditioner.

What have I gotten myself into now?

12 May 2017

Adam opens the door to the employees room, shouts at everyone in there to never ever eat or drink anything at all in his office. He slams the door shut.

He walks towards me and tells me that he is taking away half of my files. I hand him half of the bundles. He takes them and shoves them in his desk drawer.

He proceeds to count the paperclips and staples on his desk. He makes a humming sound as he counts.

"By the way Amir, do not post the paperclips with your bundles. Each paperclip costs money. The firm is losing money because of your excessive use of paperclips. Use staples instead."

01 June 2017

A call comes in from reception downstairs urgently requiring Adam. For the first time ever, Adam is not at the office. I hesitantly inform the receptionist that he is not present.

"What do you mean he is not present? He is always in. Anyways, inform him that an HMRC officer is urgently looking to sit down with him regarding his company."

Adam appears in the office half an hour after the call. I stand up and walk towards him to inform him of the serious call we got from reception.

"Sit down, Amir. HMRC are just bored. Their office is down the road so we're easy to visit."

05 June 2017

On my morning commute to work, I begin to ponder whether it is time to call it quits at Good Omen before my sanity calls quits on me. I look out at the platform and see plenty of workers in their suits on their way to work. I wonder if they all work under an Adam with a different name but have just gotten used to it. Maybe I am just a soft and sensitive individual and should wake up to the harsh reality of the legal profession. I pondered to myself silently.

In relation to my extracurricular activities, there was none now. I stopped going to the gym all together as by the time I got home, it was already closing. A gut that I previously did not have was starting to form in my midsection and forcing me to retreat to the next button on my belt.

Gamer's neck (the protrusion and jutting of the head forward) became my more natural posture as I learnt to sit and work for hours on end in silence in Adam's room, without coffee, a toilet break, or any breathers.

My cases were being stripped away from me on a day-to-day basis, and Adam was no longer providing me with a verbal reason. He would simply walk in, ask for a case, and promptly remove me as the caseworker on the matter.

I was now down to my final five cases. I felt that my time was nearing and professionally wished to finalise these cases for my personal satisfaction more than anything. I was on a sort of death row.

I presented one of my final cases to Adam and waited for the barrage of abuse. The case was in perfect condition as I conditioned myself to produce exact carbon copies of his file. After a total of four months, believe it or not, I became quite adept at producing work that resembled his after hundreds of attempts and even began mimicking his writing style.

He hummed and made croaky noises every few seconds. He then stopped, and stared at the pens at the side of his desk. He quickly leaned over, lined them up and returned to examining the file. After five minutes that felt like fifty, he crossed his arms and looked defeated. I must have won. No mistakes. Not a single one. He then quickly began sifting through the file desperately looking for a paperclip in a clear attempt to snatch a win from the jaws of defeat.

I have learnt my lesson. Not a single paperclip in sight.

"Okay, Amir. It looks fine to me. It can be dispatched now."

He hands me the file. I try to pull it out of his hands but he does not hand it over. I pull and he pulls back. He then says, "Actually, let me check one more thing."

He opens an electronic version of the file on his PC. He looks at the names of the files. Adam forced me to abbreviate files when in electronic form. For example, a payslip would be 'PS', a passport would be 'ppt'. He believed this would help "streamline" the work and make us more "efficient".

He looked at the titles of all the files line by line.

Appeal chronology. Correct. Objective material. Right. Counsel instructions. Correct. Ppt. Right. PS. Correct. BS.

"BS?!" he screamed at the top of his lungs.

"Yes, bank statements," I replied.

"Do you think you're funny, Amir? Payslips are 'PS', bank statements are 'bank statements'. Always. You never learn!" He said with a curved smile forming around his lips.

"I am taking away this file too, Amir. You have become a liability to this firm."

"But this is something that is so trivial, Adam. I actually believe you're being unprofessional here."

Adam stood up laughing. He calls the reception and tells them to bring up the security to escort me from the building as I am being uncooperative.

I walk with Adam to the lift. To explain his mood, I would say it was between ecstasy and relief.

I get into the lift with him. He stares straight at me and I get closer, resembling that of two boxers facing off.

I let rip.

"I saw you forge a client's signature and HMRC have repeatedly come to see you. Why are you avoiding them, Adam of Good Omen? What happened to that training you promised? Why have over 40 employees joined and left in a matter of weeks, and sometimes days? Forging a former client's signature? What's up with that?"

Adam's eyes turn blood shot red.

"Forging client's signature is surely a breach of sort? Is it not Adam? I have heard the Solicitors Regulation Authority take that very seriously!"

We walked towards the exit and I feel like I am about to be released from a life sentence that I was unjustly issued with.

Adam sticks out his hand and urges me to shake it. I shake his hand which was now embarrassingly limp, and squeeze his hand as hard as I can, feeling his bones crunch deep in my palm.

"See you soon, Adam".

He lets out a small whimper. "Please Amir. I do good work for people. Let's not end it like this. My business is my everything. I have nothing else."

I walk away and do not look back.

I am sure eagle eyed and legal minded readers will no doubt exclaim that I have a duty to report him. Maybe I should have reported him to the Solicitors Regulations Authority. Maybe I should have reported him to HMRC. Regardless, I was eternally relieved that I was away from it all and will never want to look back at it, and nothing will change that. Sue me.

Moreover, someone will certainly exclaim that the actions of Adam were textbook harassment and could have easily gotten him in deep waters. You must understand though that the vast majority of legal firms prey on the passion, youth, and most importantly, inexperience of recent graduates. These poor souls, I was one, will snatch at any opportunity to finally get the experience possible to put their foot through the next legal door. Some would think that escalating such issues will jeopardise their careers, making them tainted and damaged goods, or send them down a complaints rabbit-hole that will take significant time and money to resolve. Most just put it down as a bad experience and move on. Sadly the mental baggage remains for many and can later manifest itself in ways where they resemble the very people that hurt them.

4. Return of Hope

October 2017

One of the applications my wife sent off actually got a response soon after I quit. I was sitting silently in the waiting area of my local Job Centre with my mobile in my hand. I thought about playing a quick game of Sudoku whilst I wait to sign on. I see a small notification above my email. I check it and it's an email directly from a director at a quite sizeable national firm. I check the email and it is brief.

"Hi, vacancy is still open but I work in immigration, civil liberties and human rights. Are you interested in joining my team?"

I don't even wait. I reply instantly groveling at this director's feet.

I then sit down, sign on and tease the job centre worker that I won't be here for long. She doesn't find it funny.

I go home and research this firm. It did have quite an impressive history. It is one of the largest Legal Aid providers in the country, has quite renowned lawyers in the fields of immigration and public law, and a number of offices peppered across England.

The director that emailed me wasn't particularly known, and did not offer me a training contract but I was eager to sink my teeth in casework at a more sane and professional environment than Good Omens, and demonstrate skills that I have picked up.

At this point, I was beginning to get to grips with the UK's increasingly complicated immigration rules. I helped Adam's clients obtain residency, settlement and ultimately citizenship here in the UK, as well as work to establish and expand their companies. However, I was no expert yet and hoped this new place would actually provide me with some necessary training to turn me from a caseworker that is learning on the job to a solicitor in the making.

02 October 2017

I had a brief interview with the director the next day. Let's call her Yenifa. She needed a foreign language speaking caseworker anyway and had permission from up top to expand her team, which she did by hiring me.

Now, it is important to break down how a typically functioning medium to large firm here in England operates in relation to staff hierarchy and targets. I admit they are all not the same, but my experience is what matters to me.

The lowest rung position is that of a legal assistant/paralegal. They usually work harder than all those above them, are paid disgustingly meagre wages and the vast majority do not survive longer than six months. The legal assistants at this medium to large law firm were earning a salary in the region of 12,000 to 13,000GBP.

Above them lie what are known as the fee earners, composed of caseworkers, trainee solicitors, solicitors.

Caseworkers earn in the region of 15,000 to 16,000GBP (which was my salary at this place). Trainee solicitors earn 18,000 to 20,000GBP, whilst newly qualified solicitors earn between 26,000 to 30,000 (depending on the team they are in and how well they play their firm's internal politics).

As a caseworker, since I earned 15,000GBP, I had to ensure that I billed three times my salary every single month I am present – meaning I had to generate 45,000GBP for the firm by year's end.

As the vast majority of my caseload were legal aid funded files, rather than privately paid files, this made it doubly hard.

To give you a clearer understanding, if an individual walks in wanting legal assistance and qualified for legal aid, I would proceed to sign him up to the firm and prepare a legal aid form which he will sign confirming that he does not have sufficient incomes and savings, and he requires legal aid as there are merits (a low bar at this stage) to assist him with his legal matter. For this walk-in, no matter how much I do, which for an immigration case can take anywhere between 6 months to a year (sometimes a number of years) to progress fully, will only generate a "fixed fee" that we can reclaim from the Legal Aid Agency. This fixed fee amount is 413GBP. Six to twelve months of blood, sweat and tears, and I would generate 413GBP.

To compound matters, I can only claim this amount once the file is considered concluded i.e the Home Office have granted or refused this person's immigration application. As such, my work hinges on the random and opaque timing of a government department's decision-making process. I can end up doing all the work necessary, chase the government department to a level where I am sure they can take out a restraining order against me, yet not get paid, and not show the firm the money yet for the work I have done on the file.

There is one loophole in that if you do so much work that it totals three times that of the fixed fee rate (so 413 * 3 = 1248GBP), and you have charged what the Legal Aid Agency considered a "proportionate and reasonable" amount according to their lengthy Cost Assessment Guidance (that they update yearly and you are meant to be abreast and up-to-date with at all times), then you can claim the three times fixed fee amount. This is called making the file an "escape fee". Yet, the whole file has to be sent to the Legal Aid Agency after it has been concluded, with ALL evidence of work (which can surpass the size of a lever arch bundle), and they would deliberate and examine it to see if the work was properly charged. That can add a few more months to when you can finally get the actual money sent to your firm's bank account.

So, returning to my yearly target of 48,000GBP, how many fixed fee files would I have to do to generate this amount? At the very least 116 matters. So I would have to sign up 116 people over the course of a year to the firm, nine a month on average, ensure that they all qualify for legal aid with sufficient proof of means and merit, progress all their matters to a conclusion, and hope the government department, the Home Office most prominently in these cases, come to a final decision on all their matters. Then I can bill the files.

However, if you pass a three and a half hour exam demonstrating that you know all the rules and regulations concerning asylum and immigration, you can become what is considered an 'accredited caseworker'. This, combined with a Disclosure and Barring Service check, can allow you to deal with immigration and asylum matters concerning unaccompanied minors and immigrants detained in various immigration removal centres peppered around the main airports of England.

These files thankfully can generate a bit more. They are referred to as "hourly rate files" and they allow you to charge up to 800GBP worth of profit costs (essentially your financial limit on the work you do on that file) on such matters. You can do more work beyond the 800GBP barrier, however, you will need to fill out a three page Legal Aid form and explain why it is necessary and justified that you need that extra amount, and possibly add a ledger (similar to a bank statement) detailing all the work you have done to date, and predict the work you will do in the future, and estimate the cost in a neat number that won't tick off the Legal Aid Agency that you're taking the piss and want to rake in the money for the firm to meet your stringent billing targets. Incorrectly completing such a form can get you dragged in front of the Solicitors Disciplinary Tribunal.

As you can imagine, I had to undertake a gargantuan task of assisting clients almost exclusively for the purpose of trying to keep this job of 16,000GBP a year.

My first few clients I put my life and soul into, working day and night to assist them. By year's end, all I saw was a conveyor belt of 413GBPs and 800GBPs, trying to make them reach the finish line, so I can send them to the firm's billing department so they can send it to the Legal Aid Agency, so they can reply with a money bank transfer to the firm's business account. It stripped away the passion I had for "helping the helpless" – as this firm sycophantically boasts across its website and social media platforms.

To ensure caseworkers and trainee solicitors toe-the-line and generate their annual billing targets, all "work" is to be logged on a case management system, which breaks the time into the predicted money you will generate. The directors overseeing the teams will, on an almost daily basis, look at the teams times to ensure were all doing what is considered 6 to 8 hours of "chargeable" work – work that can generate the billing amount of 413GBP. Helping your client get accommodation because he is street homeless? Not chargeable. Helping your client register at a General Practice? Sorry, not chargeable. Calling him to tell him nothing has progressed in his case? Yes, that's chargeable.

The week you somehow slack and delay logging your six hours of chargeable work, for example, because you had to travel to a detention centre in Lincoln four hours away from London, then attend a Home Office minor's interview in Croydon the next day, then travel to another detention centre near Gatwick, is the week your life would be made hell. You would have your supervising solicitor coming down hard on you about your logged times, because the director came down hard on him, who in turn was warned by the billing department, who are all under immense pressure from the untouchable CEO who made it a crime to ever fall below six hours of daily chargeable work. Unfortunately, this modus operandi exists in almost all firms up and down the country.

November 2017

I slowly begin to acquaint myself with various members of my new team. I start to realise an invisible string that extends across all legal practices I worked in: mental instability among working staff. I have my theories about it. One of those theories is that those of a positive disposition are ultimately pushed out of the door by the sheer brute of the work, the constant nagging, the Machiavellian colleagues, the dictatorial director, and so on. The ones that do stay on are slowly jaded to the point that they turn into human zombies. Clocking in at 8am, leaving at 8pm, and repeating this cycle until they burn out completely or retire early. As such, the nice guys are far and few between.

What is common are young fee earners, ready to snap your neck and steal your wallet to ensure they remain ahead and in front, ready to be 'recognised' by a senior staff member and reap some rewards, from being given a training contract to commence as a trainee solicitor, or to simply be a known face in their small legal bubble. These exist in the abundance of nitrogen in the Earth's atmosphere.

Though the most painful common element, and the most clichéd unfortunately, is that the most conniving, cut-throat colleagues do time and again rise to the top of the food chain. From Adam, being able to churn enough clients to build his own firm and rinse out young graduates, to the directors at this national firm, to Yennifa, who gives off an air of a bubbly nursery school teacher masking something much harsher underneath.

Hilariously, these characters if in the same environment do clash between each other. Following the collapse of a fierce national rival (due allegedly to a sex scandal involving the CEO), this national firm that I was at ended up absorbing the collapsed firm's most senior and experienced staff.

The layout of my work floor is that of a chicken farm. Rows of table, with each row being controlled by a director and his/her team. The floor consisting of maybe 20 to 30 teams. The amount of fee earners present in a confined space clearly extended beyond that stipulated by health and safety regulations, that when I extend my mouse a bit too far right, I accidentally end up touching the hand of my supervisor – who is clearly used to the cramped style and ignores me.

Anyway, a director at the collapsed firm ended up joining our bank due to the lack of available tables. Yennifa did not like that. It was tantamount to a silverback gorilla having its territory invaded. Yennifa's tone turns sour as she now demands everyone in the bank to work in silence, whilst the rest of the floor scream at the top of their lungs like a stock exchange trading floor.

Yennifa slowly begins to ramp up her aggression. In the weekly Monday morning meeting to assess our chargeable work, she makes it the top agenda to inform her of any "weird things this stuck up director" says or does. Colleagues in the team enter pack mode and they regularly begin to exchange funny or awkward encounters they had with this unassuming director.

"She printed too many bundles in colour. Surely that's not allowed?" one pipes up.

"I think she likes this colleague. I saw her talk to him twice," another jumps in gleefully enjoying the gossip.

The agenda for the Monday meeting ultimately reached a conclusion that we must "work together" to stave off the invasion of this director. A war call for something so mundane as a new director sitting on our bank of tables.

We go back to our desks. Yennifa promptly demands of the new director to keep her voice down as it's giving her a migraine. Sniggering among our bank spreads. The new director turns red and apologises. One nil to Yennifa.

December 2017

Yennifa comes in fuming from a meeting with the CEO. Apparently, the new director will have her own team soon and they can also sit with us.

Yennifa takes us out for an urgent team lunch. She swears like a soldier, calling this new director every derogative under the sun. Yennifa starts to go paranoid, whispering to us that the CEO might actually be planning to sack us all, and the new director has fluttered her eyelashes at him and is going to send us all packing.

Yennifa begins to conclude that the only way she can stop this and save us all is if she takes her out and there's a "spatter of arterial blood across the walls and ceiling of this firm".

We conclude the lunch and she demands us to pay for the lunch she called us to and to tip the waiters.

"I can't pay for all ten of you," she says as she walks out, gets into her latest model Range Rover Vogue and speeds off home.

The following day she stands up straight and points between the eyes of the director, and signals to her to come upstairs to speak to the CEO. They vanish beyond the corridors into the lift. Yennifer comes down in a triumphant mood. She tells the new director's team of three to piss off from our bank. Orders directly from the effing CEO, she says.

The new director and her new staff begin their migration. Where to, you say? One bank behind us. This, according to Yennifa, is a win up there with David's triumph over Goliath. I struggle to see it, but I keep my mouth firmly shut and log my six hours of chargeable work, and call it a day before Yennifa makes an example out of me.

22 December 2017

I check my watch awaiting the end of the day. Time has slowed down to snail pace. My mind has already wandered off in to the weekend and Christmas festivities are playing in my mind. I push the thought of returning to the office before the New Year out of the front of my mind. A demand from Yennifa to all junior staff to "cover" senior solicitors work while they're off between Christmas and New Year.

"The courts keep churning on and on!", she would say. No, they do not actually but let's not get bogged down with details.

An email comes in from the trainee at the rival bank of tables.

"Hey everyone,

My client's passport and BRP is lost somewhere in the office. She is from Finland. Has anyone seen it?"

A few moments later, I turn around to see her quietly sobbing at the printers.

I decide to send her a funny email to cheer her up.

"Hey,

I'm sure you'll find it! The admin team return in a few days time and they will help.

But if they don't, you're all but Finnish'ed.

Kind regards,

Amir"

She returns to her desk and I assume reads my email. Her soft sobbing turns into outright wailing. I pack my things hurriedly and scamper to the exit.

January 2018

Dispersed between the bitter rivalries of director on director, solicitor against solicitor, and trainee against trainee, are some things called your own actual cases. Surprisingly, every now and again you remember your role of helping these poor individuals with their cases.

A hunched man came through our door asking for help. As usual, the junior staff like myself are sent to see them and see how we can fleece them for money first before deciding if Legal Aid is applicable in their circumstance.

He begins to explain to me that his building was on fire, that he had to run for his life, and that he is homeless, whilst his wife remains in Iran, unable to come to the UK despite being pregnant with his child and being married for many years.

He pushes some muddled papers at me. I read them nonchalantly but then I realise that his case is as serious as he says it is. I start to read more intently, seeing summaries of doctor's note with "mental breakdown" scrawled on them, other letters explaining "dislocation of shoulder" and "injuries to back attempting to escape inferno of building".

I realise that this individual is a survivor of the Grenfell Tower fire. On 14 June 2017, a fire broke out in the 24-storey Grenfell Tower block of flats in North Kensington, West London. It caused at least 72 deaths as far as official figures go. The British Government seem to not recognise that many were asylum seekers living in that block due to no alternative accommodation being provided, yet not counted among the dead. It was the deadliest structural fire in the United Kingdom since 1988.

The man begins to break down. He whimpers that he just wants to see his wife and baby.

"That's all I want, nothing more," as tears stream down his face.

I realise that due to the injuries he obtained trying to escape the building, he is now disabled with severe shoulder and back issues. Mental health issues torment him with nightmares and persistent insomnia. His finances are barely existent, as he now lives in a hostel provided by the local authority as they attempt to find him a suitable alternative accommodation. He no doubt qualifies for legal aid and I intend to do what I dreamt of doing when I entered this profession, to help those in need seek justice and closure.

I quickly go up to my desk and speak to my supervisor. He realises that this is a potentially good case, and urges me to sign him up and progress his matter as quick as possible to find a way to bring over his pregnant wife. A colleague sitting close by chips in.

"Make sure you charge him some money," she says almost automatically, rubbing her index and thumb together.

Another hears the word Grenfell.

"Hey Amir, let me take conduct of this case, you can help me". A squabble breaks out amongst two senior solicitors in the team. Yennifa looks on happy to see her war dogs fight among themselves for new meat. She does not intervene.

I hold firm and take full conduct of the case.

To progress the matter, I get into contact with the International Red Cross. They manage to track down the client's wife in Iran since he has lost contact with her when his whole flat went up in flames, along with mobile and telephone numbers. They manage to track her down in some rural area in Iran.

I prepare a visit visa application and bleed my heart out urging the UK Visas & Immigration (UKVI) to allow her in, despite her being from a country usually unable to get entry clearance. I add in at the end that this is a case involving heightened media attention, and we do not want this to escalate into a public and litigious affair. They grant the visa.

The client and his wife are united. He comes in with his heavily pregnant wife to thank me. I tell him the battle is not over. We must now find a way to get her to stay. I begin preparation of an in-country further leave application. I explain that the UKVI have raised the prices of application (again). It now costs in the region of 1033GBP (at the time) and further 1000GBP for something called the Health Surcharge (so that they can have access to the NHS). At time of writing, this has also gone up. The client is on various social benefits. He is not financially minted, and will obviously find it difficult to stump up 2033GBP in the space of a few months before his wife's six months visit visa elapses.

I attempt to do what is called a Home Office fee waiver, explaining that the client is not in a financially stable position with the whole burning of his entire flat situation, and forking out such an amount will cause him hardship. They reject this, explaining in a simple paragraph that basically he gets benefits and is living in a hostel, as he is not what you would consider "destitute" and can "utilise" the current social support he gets to pay for the application.

I explain to the client that we can try to challenge this. Unsurprisingly, he is not willing to risk the status of his wife turning into that of a visa 'overstayer' (a black mark on a person's immigration history that can have devastating consequences on future applications), so he calls a friend all but begging him for a loan of 2033GBP. The friend thankfully provides this.

I begin compiling various evidence demonstrating that to send the wife home is akin to causing intense suffering and hardship, tearing the family unit apart, and the client will not be able to relocate with his wife back in Iran. I start reading the reports I obtain from his GP, counsellors, and specialists. I realise painfully that although legal firms see these individuals as nothing more than moneybags, each client holds a unique story and many times have their life teetering on the edge of despair. I begin to read the latest medical report explaining how the client attempted to overdose on medication soon after he escaped the building, and how he can barely lift his arms or turn his neck. His depression level on their medical scale is at the highest it can be, prior to the arrival of his wife.

I start developing my legal argument researching and incorporating case after case demonstrating that there exists legal precedent allowing the client's wife to stay in the UK, despite being only a short-term visit visa, does not speak English, and does not have a property to permanently house her in (for obvious reasons).

I send it off to the UKVI. Three long months later, I finally get a decision. I rip open the decision letter. I see a Biometric Residence Permit confirming the client's wife's status in the UK as an individual with leave to remain for two and half years. Joy fills me as I rush to inform the client. I call and inform him of the good news. He tells me to repeat it three more times, because he can't believe it. I celebrate with my supervisor who looks on proudly. I ask my supervisor whether we have to do this application all over again in two and a half years. He says yes, that we have to repeatedly do it to cover 10 years of continuous presence in the UK, and only then will she qualify to remain here indefinitely. I ask if the client has to keep paying 2033GBP every time. He says yes, and that the prices are likely to go up every April by the UKVI as it has turned into good business for them. He breaks this moment by urging me to "just celebrate this big achievement, you did well."

Yennifa walks by. She is also happy but for a different reason.

"Proceed to bill this file as you're behind on your billing and bringing the team total down. Three times your salary is the minimum every month, remember?"

April 2018

A colleague from our team that sits opposite me recently had her birthday. She has installed her birthday balloons on her desk. Her desk, like the rest of the bank, are within centimetres of each other. I politely ask her to remove one particular balloon, which repeatedly falls and blocks my computer screen. She tells me to shut up.

One week goes by and the balloons thankfully begin to shrink. I'm hoping by the end of the week, they'll be small enough for me to see my full screen. I decide since the one blocking my screen is already half-inflated I might as well squeeze the rest of the air from it. I hold on to it and squeeze slightly but it ends up popping.

The colleague turns to me with venomous eyes.

"Amir, I will knock you out right now."

She squares up to me in a boxer's stance. I tell her to sit down. She gets in my face ready to enter a full-on brawl. I don't move and look her square in the eyes. She finally backs down.

She then demands the banks to be rearranged because she says she's "seconds away from killing this little rat." I think she meant me.

One day later, the order of the banks are being rearranged by Yennifa who enjoyed listening in to this little fracas without intervening.

This time she puts me next to the loudest and most confrontational colleague in the team. Every single team member refused to sit next to her, and urged Yennifa not to do it. Yennifa declares to all that Amir will sit next to her as I allegedly have a "calm demeanour" and can "handle" her, the way I handled the balloons-loving colleague. How she managed to reach that decision seeing someone square up to me over a half-inflated balloon, and decides to pair me with another maniac, is reasoning that only Yennifa will know the wisdom behind.

May 2018

I begin to realise that the only way I am going to work my way out of being a lowly caseworker and into contention to being a trainee solicitor at this firm is to sit that exam that, if I pass, will allow me to work cases of individuals in detention centres and unaccompanied minors.

To do so, I had to sit a three and half hour exam called the Law Society Immigration and Asylum Accreditation Scheme.

Building up to the exam, I asked if I am eligible for some sort of exam leave. The flat answer from HR was 'no'. I had to use my own annual leave and pay the exam fee myself, and if I passed it, they will reimburse me the exam fee. At 15,000GBP a year, roughly a grand a month in net pay a month, in expensive London, coughing up 500GBP was no easy task. Truly without the facility of an overdraft, none of my travel to the office would have been possible for the month.

I sit down with Yennifa a week before the exam. I ask her whether me passing this exam will result in me being rewarded with a training contract since I have developed my caseload, will bring in a ton of new cases (that will be charged under an hourly rate basis, rather than fixed fee), and will in turn benefit the firm greatly. She leans in, looks me straight into my soul, and proclaims that I will definitely be given a training contract, and that she will see to it to the "ends of the Earth".

The word of the director. Surely that is an unbreakable bond.

I fly out of the room and return to my desk. I clock in six hours of chargeable work, head home and begin to study throughout the night for the accreditation exam.

A week flies past and I prepare myself to be questioned on any and every aspect of the UK's immigration rules and legislation. In theory, I have enough knowledge up in my noggin to take the place of an Upper Tribunal judge. I head to the exam venue and see a few of my colleagues there who are also sitting this exam. One tells me that he has attempted it twice, and this is his third attempt. Third time lucky I say. I ask another if this is her first time. She replies saying it is only her second, but she says she is quietly optimistic this time as Yennifa printed off helpful answers and templates and stuck them on the back of some her statute books. I do not ask if this is allowed.

I sit the exam and the three and a half hours fly past. I feel completely rinsed with every aspect of immigration law questioned, extending at points to include ethical questions, client care and drafting skills.

They inform us that we will get our results in a few weeks. Those few weeks pass by as I count each day, hoping upon hope that I can pass this exam and put myself in the driving seat towards being a trainee.

On results day, I refresh the exam board page again and again, waiting for the result to appear. It finally does. I have passed it, and so have my two other colleagues! I stand up and punch the air in happiness. My colleague who attempted the exam three times, calls his mum and cries to her over the phone, exclaiming that he is going to become a trainee solicitor.

My supervisor stands up and gives me a brotherly hug. Even Yennifa is happy as she goes and congratulates the one colleague she stuck the answers to the back of her statute book.

Myself and third-time-lucky colleague go up to her and ask her when we will commence our training contracts. She explains that she has gotten the ball rolling on the training contract of the colleague that had the answers stuck to her statute book. As for me and Mr. Attempt Number Three, we have to wait while she "sweet talks the CEO". Confusion pierces the cloud of happiness as this is the first time we have heard that the CEO had to be sweet-talked into giving us a training contract, but we both brush it off and await the approval of our training contracts.

Due to my newly obtained stripes, I am now immediately trusted to handle immigration and asylum cases that involve detained clients (located in detention centres and Her Majesty's prisons), as well as unaccompanied asylum-seeking minors. My initial anticipation that I would be eased into it evaporated within days, as my DBS check came through rapidly, and Yennifa dumped my colleague's difficult and unwanted cases on my desk so I can sharpen my teeth.

Within hours, I was hitting the M1 with my 2004 Vauxhall Corsa, to Lincolnshire, to see my first detained client in Morton Hall Immigration Removal Centre. Approximately a three hour drive from London, with the detention centre being a former prison turned immigration centre. I get searched and searched again. I am moved from one station to the next, requiring to demonstrate sufficient ID, clear my pockets, and have my tie and collar repeatedly checked. You would think I was about to see Hannibal Lecter.

I am sat down by a guard at a desk with the chairs drilled into the ground and tables stuck to the wall. Behind me runs a thin red wire that I am to press if I feel threatened or in danger. I am told to await the arrival of my client. We shall call him Mr. Farah.

Mr. Farah appears at the door. A long shadow is drawn across the room. I slowly turn around to see him, my legs slightly vibrating. Mr. Farah stares me down. My nervousness instantly evaporates as a small 5ft nothing scrawny young man sticks his hand out to shake. I extend my hand back and introduce myself. He then proceeds to bop around the table, sticks one leg on the chair, and tucks his hand into his groin area for comfort. The last part disgusted me and I was desperate to wash my hands but it was my first case.

"So when are you going to buss me out of this place? Man is about to crack in here, you get me?"

I start to take a detailed immigration history of Mr. Farah and try to understand what we should challenge in order to get this individual his liberty and his previous leave to remain in the UK reinstated, which was revoked by the Home Office due to his criminality. I identify the relevant legislation which the Home Office have relied on to detain and issue removal proceedings against him. I tried to transform all that theory that swirled in my head into practical steps and advice, with no sample, no previous experience and no training pumped into me to prepare me for this. Simply my revision notes and Mr. Farah.

As I delved deeper into his story, looking at various papers he later brought in that he brandished in front of me, the case appeared as follows. Mr. Farah was a Somali national that fled with his aunt and brothers during the height of the Somali civil war in the early nineties. Mr. Farah was only two years old at the time and does not recall anything. He came to the UK and was granted asylum status as a dependent to his aunt. He attended school, learnt English (which was now his main language), made friends and had fights. He was diagnosed with ADHD early on and struggled to focus in class. His aunt attempted to discipline him by burning him with an iron, hitting him with a coat hanger, and soon resorting to strangling him with a wire. He was identified by his scars around his neck in school and was quickly taken in by social services. His aunt was prosecuted and he never saw her again.

His ADHD morphed to include anxiety. His anger became uncontainable and fights became a regular theme in his life.

He pushed on to actually attend Sixth Form college with a dream of becoming a mechanic, but he was evidently a man with many problems. He began selling weed to his peers. This snowballed into distribution of Class A and B drugs and affray on the streets of West London. This resulted in stints in various juvenile prisons all before he turned 18.

He was fast approaching the age of 18. He was a boy that had no parents, his siblings went their separate way, and his aunt who brought him up, who then brought him down, was gone forever. He had a girlfriend but it appeared that she was looking for the exit door out of his troubled life.

Mr. Farah obtained indefinite leave to remain following the grant of his refugee status when he was a child, but in the eyes of the law he was not a British national – rather an individual with 'settled' status. This settled status turns quickly to unsettled chaos.

Mr. Farah's trajectory though was obvious. The moment he turned 18, he was involved in an altercation, he began carrying various knives and the London Metropolitan Police busted him in no time. First crime as an adult.

Mr. Farah was sent to one of Her Majesty's finest prisons, the dingy Brixton Prison in South London, and served half his time. He was set to be released on licence for the remainder of his sentence due to good behaviour and undertaking of various extracurricular activities demonstrating a redeemed young man on a path to redemption. With him setting a foot firmly outside the walls of the prison, UK immigration authorities swooped him up and drove him to this middle-of-nowhere detention centre three hours from London.

His leave to remain in the country was revoked due to his criminality. He was informed in writing that the Home Office intend to deport him to Somalia, his country of origin – a country he doesn't remember, barely speaks the language, and has not stepped foot in since his escape as a two year old close to two decades ago.

Thinking about this now, it is interesting how the Home Office has reasoned this. No doubt some readers would think that a foreign national criminal should not be roaming the streets of the UK, and that he should be taken to where he came from to be dealt with as he is not our headache. This is understandable but incredibly naïve. Let us take Mr. Farah himself as an example. He was abused by his aunt here in the UK and required to be strangled before the social services woke up and realised what was going on. He became a drugs dealer here in the UK. He committed every single one of his crimes in the UK. He speaks English as his main language. He supports an English football club (a terrible one but we will skirt over it). He watches English television shows from Eastenders to Mock the Week. He had an English girlfriend. He was as English as afternoon tea. Yet here he was, being treated as a foreign national criminal and being threatened with deportation to a land as alien to him as it is to me. No doubt, he was an unsavoury character, but this was farcical. Even beyond Mr. Farah, the Home Office's modus operandi for every single foreign national criminal is roughly the same. Commit a crime, lose your status, prepare to be deported. A one size fits all, regardless of whether you came here last night or last decade, that you have your whole family here or just a pet. The legislation governing this was surprisingly introduced by a Labour Government, and neatly titled the UK Borders Act 2007, with the specifics articulated under section 33.

Now, we can provide reasons within weeks of being served with a notice of deportation for why you should stay in this country. A mere few weeks to beg a caseworker in the Home Office's Immigration Enforcement team, who is likely never going to talk to you throughout the whole process or come to see you, as to why you have developed such a deep and meaningful life here in the UK and that they should not tear you out by your roots and throw you into another country to deal with you and your criminal ways.

After you have provided them with document upon document of supporting evidence showing that you are rehabilitating, taking anger classes, demonstrating you were a clever student back in school, that you had a girlfriend and siblings and friends, that you are remorseful, and that you are struggling with various mental health issues, they will likely refuse it with a 10 page copy and paste job sprinkled with a few stale arguments by the Home Office caseworker. The caseworker usually has cut-and-paste refutation for every aspect of human life. You have a girlfriend? She can visit you in Somalia. You have siblings? They can come along to Somalia too with your girlfriend. You were academically okay in school? You committed too many crimes to demonstrate that you truly cared, and if anything, you can use those qualifications to find a job there. Finally, you say you have mental health issues? Here's a seven year old Somalia country report picked up from Google stating that Somalia has mental health facilities. Good luck. Send us a post card. This style, this conveyer belt style of refusal, existed in every single one of my deportation cases.

After working and essentially wasting our time with the Home Office, I advise Mr. Farah that we must appeal this decision and go to the First-tier Tribunal for an independent judge to determine. He agrees but is now seriously waning in detention. He has been there for seven months. Bail application after bail application was made. Refused every time due to his criminal history. Here, I have no qualms but I still did not feel leaving him in a prison-turned-immigration centre was the right environment for a reforming young man to be in – let alone for seven months when technically he had no outstanding criminal sentence.

I have appointment after appointment with Mr. Farah over the coming months to prepare him for his appeal. Every time I see him he is a little more withdrawn, and little more thin. You won't pick up on it the first time, but then it slowly becomes evident. His eyes are a little more baggy, his tone a little more quiet. He had the same routine questions asking about when he will be released and exclaiming that he is not a criminal anymore, but something was happening to him. In my last attendance with him, he was completely still and dazed for most of it. He says he was put on medication but can't remember the name. I ask the staff to provide me with his full medical records. I am told I will get it within a few weeks. I hope I get it in time for the hearing. I ask for a guarantee. They say they are understaffed and to chase it in writing.

Finally, a hearing is listed in the First-tier Tribunal (the court dealing with his immigration matter) and a barrister is hired to carry out the advocacy in court. The day comes and I desperately want to see Mr. Farah out of detention to help him reintegrate into society. I am called from the privately owned company that is hired to transport detainees to prison. There has been an issue with Mr. Farah. I ask the man on the phone to clarify. He tells me to get into contact with the relevant team in the Home Office. What is the relevant team? He hangs up.

The Home Office presenting officer (legal officer attending court on behalf of the Home Office) is equally as confused and simply walks off to a corner of the court not to be harassed.

I leaf through paper after paper trying to find a contact detail for the Immigration Enforcement team dealing with his case. I call and each number is either out of order, or the telephone operator gives me a number to another section of the department. I am bounced around but finally get through to the case owner driving Mr. Farah's terrors on the other side. I ask her about Mr. Farah, she isn't aware of the name. Finally after providing her with his date of birth, nationality, Home Office reference, and other personal details she has a light bulb moment.

"Aha, Mr. Farah in Morton Hall? I was meaning to update you. He was being disruptive on transport."

"What do you mean?" I scream.

"Well, in my notes it appears he has tried to take his own life but this is not confirmed so don't quote me on it."

Hearing is adjourned.

June 2018

One of the placement providers for unaccompanied asylum-seeking children has contacted our firm and require legal representatives to assist with their asylum claims.

I am allocated a Sudanese minor. I ask Yennifa if I can first shadow a senior colleague to see how to run this type of case. Yennifa smiles and begins exuding an air of friendliness – similar to a primary school teacher or motherly aunt.

"It's quite simple Amir – it's like any other asylum claim but be a bit nicer to them. Good luck!"

Okay, first thing's first. I have to have an initial attendance with them which can last anything between one to three hours to take in their story, immigration history, and to advise them of all the steps that are likely to take place up until a decision is made by the Home Office.

After that, I will have to book them at the Asylum Intake Unit in Croydon. Unlike adults, I have to persuade their social worker to do it and then attend with them all as well.

I plan to meet the minor and his social worker at the entrance of the Home Office Croydon building. I also instruct an independent interpreter to attend (covered by Legal Aid) to help with interpreting if the Home Office interpreter cocks up – which they usually do.

I make my journey to East Croydon and I am at the entrance at 8:59am. Screening interviews, which are the first interview an asylum seeker will have to do, do not last any longer than 15 minutes. I expect to be in and out of there in no time.

We all get searched and make our way to the second floor. There is no reception. I do not see a single Home Office employee, but many asylum-seeking children. There are cameras at all four corners of this room. I do not want to demonstrate to the social worker or the independent interpreter that I do not know what I am meant to do at this point.

I go drink a sip of water. I then sit down and pretend to look through some urgent notes. The social worker leans in and tells me politely to stand up and go knock on a door near the entrance.

I look at the door and it says "Home Office" scrawled on a laminated paper. I go up and knock. Time elapses and no one emerges. I knock again. Nothing. I go to sit back down and I am now truly confused. The social worker huffs and storms up to the door and bangs on it loudly. A bald employee with glasses that can turn upwards opens the door and hands her a little slip with a number on it.

"Wait for this number to be called out," He squeaked. Then he shut the door hard in her face.

She gave it to me and explained that I am to take the minor to the room that will be called out in the next few hours. Hours? I surely must have misheard, so I proceed to ignore this.

The independent interpreter begins to walk around. He is bored and he is making it obvious.

I begin to talk to the minor to try to cheer him up and change his mood. He surely must be feeling stressed with this burden at such a young age. Surprisingly, he is upbeat and is happy to be in the UK, and the fact that he has been given new clothes and clothing allowance by the foster family he has been allocated to.

The interpreter then sits down and takes out his phone, and begins playing a game of Soduku on it.

The camera suddenly shifted in the corner near the Home Office door. The bald man bursts out in to the room and storms to us.

"You cannot use your phone here. Look at the sign on the door!" he booms.

"Sorry, I didn't know. I will put it away now," the interpreter apologetically blurts as he becomes visibly uncomfortable.

"That will not do. Leave the building now or I will call security. You have compromised all the minors in this room."

"No, sir. I am sorry. I put it away."

"No can do. Leave now or I will call security."

The Home Office employee took out his walkie talkie and called security.

The interpreter, myself and the social worker were shocked. The minor's excitement to be wearing new clothes was wiped out. This is my first time here. I did not know if I can even do anything here.

"I want to speak to your manager then," The interpreter interjected.

"I am the bloody manager! Now leave!" the Home Office officer exclaimed.

The interpreter realising what a stir this has caused apologises to me and the minor and makes his way out.

The Home Office officer then looks around and wags his finger at everybody.

"Anybody found to be using his phone will have the same fate. Security will be called and you will be taken out."

He then walked back triumphantly to the Home Office door and vanished within.

Two hours elapse and we are still waiting. I lean over to the social worker and ask her how long this will take.

She leans back and says "hours, like I told you."

Looks like I didn't mishear anything. True to her words, 5 and a half hours later, the minor and I were finally called in to have his biometric data enrolled and then to have a small ten minute interview to take his basic details.

We waited a further hour to get copies of all the paperwork.

In total, we waited six and a half hours for a ten minute interview and some fingerprints to be taken.

July 2018

Yennifa has had a meeting with the CEO. Since I obtained my accreditation, I have been regularly querying her about the status of my training contract. She would put me off politely with an acceptable excuse.

"As soon as I corner the CEO, I will put in the word."

"Remind me on Friday and I see what I can do."

"Put in a word with HR on this and quote me on it."

I followed her instructions to the letter. I began a chain of emails with HR explaining that I am waiting for my training contract update.

I see new people join and the internal intranet's front page congratulating the newbies on their "well deserved training contracts".

I sit with Attempt-Number-Three, let's call him James, in the food court as we eat a cold hotdog and fries. He is at boiling point as he bites violently down on his food. He castigates and laments our situation, explaining that the world is going by, new employees are joining, starting their training contracts and moving up, whilst we lounge waiting for the CEO to cast his mighty eye on us. He works himself up into a storm and decides that he will track the HR manager himself and ask that he passes on a request to the CEO to consider his training contract prospects.

He then manages to call up the HR team and corner the HR manager whilst he is on the way to lunch. He has a meeting and the HR manager agrees to pass on the message to the CEO. He actually ends up passing the message to Yennifa.

As we sat down to continue getting our six hours per day chargeable work, Yennifa storms in and screams at James at the top of her lungs.

"How dare you try to go behind my back to get a training contract?! I decide when you get one!" She slams her fists on his desk.

James retorts back calmly saying, "I will not talk to you while you are speaking to me in this tone" and continues typing away calmly on his computer.

"Come outside now, James!" Yennifa is getting closer and closer to his face, reaching to about a foot away.

He ignores her. She then walks back to her desk and types violently at her keyboard.

For the first time ever I have seen the chattering loud office go dead silent.

Yennifa sends out an email to the team and demands that everyone demonstrates to her by the end of the day that they have logged six hours or no one is to go home.

I log my hours and leave the office in a hurry.

The next day, James and Yennifa are both early to the office. I come in and the environment is toxic. Yennifa isn't talking to anyone in the team and neither is James. James proceeds to print out a letter and leaves it on Yennifa's desk. He tells her that he is handing in his notice today and thanks her for the opportunity.

She sulks and says, "I am so done with immature boys", and tosses the sheet away from her.

James served his final month as per his contract. The firm's billing report for the financial year comes in and everyone is listed in some sort of leaderboard of who billed what and how much. If your name is the in red, you have billed less than three times your salary – and that you should expect some sort of official meeting with your team director and maybe the untouchable high-at-top CEO. If your name is in the green, you have successfully billed three times your salary and you will likely be rewarded by being dumped more cases. You will not get any sort of bonus if you go beyond, not even a thank you email.

My name was in red and my gut suddenly turned. My salary was 15,000 and have billed only 35,000, just over two times my salary. James' name is in green and he has billed just under

50,000 and he is on the same salary as me. A hard worker about to be let go.

He gets an email at this point and calls me over.

"Hey Amir, look, I leave tomorrow and the CEO has finally responded to me. He is willing to offer me a training contract that starts next year."

I urge him to take it but he is adamant that enough is enough and he has found another firm that is willing to take him on immediately.

I understand his point of view and pat him in a platonic manner.

Yennifa then drops me an email. 'Meeting at 12' it says. I wait nervously to 12pm and she escorts me to a meeting room. She is pleasant again with the façade of a friendly child minder.

"Amir, I have spoken to the CEO and you have not hit your targets. We're going to have to give you more cases to hopefully boost your billing. Is that okay with you?"

I state the only thing I can, and that is that I agree. I want to drop the training contract question but after seeing James get verbally bludgeoned for it, I decide to leave it for another time.

I work tirelessly for the next three months in the hope of churning out enough money for the firm for the CEO to cast his eyes at me. By around the end of August 2018, I had successfully hit three times my salary for each month. I would come in at 8am, work until 12pm, make my way to a detention centre to see client after client, then make my way back and work until 7pm. I did this day after day. My supervisor was worried and came over for a friendly chat.

"Don't work yourself to death. Trust me, you don't want to have a head like mine," He laughed as he pointed at his balding head.

"If he dies, he dies," I quote Ivan Drago from Rocky IV. We both laugh and then back to the zombie typing to get our six hours of chargeables, or Yennifa would come down on us like a ton of bricks.

The end of August arrives and Yennifa has hired another addition to the team to replace James. She is a polite and eager individual and she has just graduated.

Yennifa introduces her to us as a team.

"Team, this is Priscilla. She graduated from Cardiff University and is now joining our team. She is the newest trainee solicitor in our team and I am very happy for her. Do not give her any work involving minors or detention as she is not a level 2 senior caseworker yet and she has little working knowledge at the moment, but I have no doubt that she will pass it soon."

Talk about pouring salt in the wound. Make no mistake, I have nothing against Priscilla. She seemed like a wonderful person and she managed to figure out a way to walk through the door and be handed a training contract from the get go. But I truly was mindboggled about how to persuade Yennifa to do the same for me. What else can I do?

I wait to find Yennifa in a quiet corner and go up to her. I urged her as politely as possible to see whether a training contract is on the horizon for me. My supervisor backed me by providing a long email explaining to her why I am ready to start a training contract.

She stares at me and then something computes behind her eyes and she smiles.

"If I see the CEO's Mercedes parked outside, I will approach him."

Okay, new mission. I have to wait for the CEO to drive in to his parking spot. I regularly made trips to the printer to take a peak at his parking spot from the window. After four days checking, he finally made a visit to our branch.

I skipped to Yennifa like Dorothy down Yellow Brick Road, in the hope of finally seeing the man behind the curtain granting me my wish of a training contract.

Yennifa is cornered now. She has to go and talk to him which she slowly does. Before she returns, an email pops up on my screen. It is from the CEO's secretary with the title "Intent to give you Training Contract".

I quickly read it and see that the CEO has signed a letter explaining that if I continue to get six hours of chargeable hours every day and hit three times my salary in billing every month until November, then in December I will officially start my training contract!

I punch the air in joy. My supervisor shakes my hand. My colleagues congratulate me. I am ecstatic, overjoyed, delighted. I call my wife and she is equally as happy. Training contract means career progression, which means an improved salary than 15,000, which means we can finally move out of our studio apartment and into something slightly bigger. That day every colour was bright, every ray of sunshine was divine. I was floating on cloud nine.

From September to November, I continued to work fingers to the bone. I did not want to leave anything down to chance. I must get six hours of chargeable work. I must bill three times my salary. I was stacking cases on cases. The quality of my work was no doubt dwindling as I yearned to progress and bill as many cases as possible. Client being deported back to a war-torn "country of origin"? Not my problem anymore. Push the file into the billing basket. My supervisor took me aside and explained that my work is okay but I am no longer spending time with my clients, not being as thorough and careful as I used to, not researching new points of law and caselaw to get an upper hand on the Home Office, and risk seeing clients as mere numbers. I retort back sharply saying "the firm only cares about how much money you make them. I have to stack them high and sell them cheap."

As I blurted that, something in me died but I refused to look away.

His eyes were sad and the disappointment alone spoke to my soul, but my eyes were firmly on the prize now. There was no way around it. If I carefully progress each case, I would not be able to bill as much. It was I would say mutually exclusive at that point.

November quickly came and I check my records. Seven to eight hours every single day from September until November – not counting admin tasks which add a further two hours. No sick days taken. No annual leave used. Just printing money on money. However, my billing was high but fluctuated over those three months. September and October were fine, but November was slightly lower than three times my salary due to many cases simply waiting on a decision by the Home Office and the Tribunals. I allay my own fears by reasoning that no one rational would hang up my entire training contract on a blip, which is totally out of my control.

December 2018

The first week of December rumbles on. I receive no update from my director, Yennifa, or the human resources department. On the Friday before going home I decide to send out a barrage of emails to the new worker in the human resources. She replies.

Incoming email. Title of email: Revocation of Training Contract offer.

"Dear Amir,

Thank you for your email.

Due to inconsistent **_actual_** billing during the months' observation, we have decided to revoke our training contract offer.

Note that actual billing differs from chargeable work (also known as billable work). Your chargeables may not necessarily translate to actual billing.

If you need further assistance with billing files, please speak to your supervisor.

Kind regards"

My heart felt like it dropped into the mouth of a volcano and incinerated down to its particles. My eyes water and my legs shake nervously. I turn to my supervisor who begins to read it. He is visibly distressed.

I walk up to Yennifa. Before I even speak she replies, "I know about the revocation of the training contract offer. Go air your grievances to HR."

I begin to stutter and splutter, trying to will her to step in and help me here. She pouts her lips and shrugs.

I go upstairs and locate the HR department's room. A pin code is installed on the door which prevents anyone from walking in on them. I bang the door repeatedly until the new HR worker comes to the door. I stick my foot in and demand that I speak about the training contract revocation.

She can see I am in a serious mood and enters into a psychiatrist persona, that we should sit down and discuss this calmly and professionally. She offers me tea and coffee, I ignore.

I let rip at her in a fifteen-minute diatribe. I break down all my numbers, my work, my sacrifices to reach their unattainable targets. I cut her up and speak over her again and again. I begin to realise that I am venting simply at a pawn in this whole game. That what it boils down to is simply the man upstairs.

She gets an email pop up in her inbox from my supervisor who I read off the screen appears to have already written a two page email urging a reconsideration on my behalf.

I tell her that I want to speak to the CEO now. She tells me it is not possible and that he is in meetings the whole week, and visiting other branches the next.

I demand that a reconsideration is made in 48 hours. She said she will pass on my message.

I go back to my desk and Yennifa appears behind me like a zombie ascending from an ancient grave.

"I said air your grievances to me so I can air it to HR!" she screams at the top of her lungs.

Other teams on other banks of table turn around to the spectacle she appears to be making before returning to a dull chatter of keyboard sounds and mouse clicks.

I tell her that she specifically told me to air my grievances to HR just a few minutes ago. My supervisor jumps in and affirms this.

She goes back to her desk, picks up the phone, and starts a conversation with a client of hers on the phone as if nothing has happened. She leans back and cackles as the conversation I assume must have turned to a funny anecdote.

After a period of melancholy and defeat, I begin to have a series of realisations. I am not the smartest worker in the block but I try hard, very hard. I have completed my legal studies, and accredited as a senior caseworker demonstrating a higher than usual level of expertise. I surely must be attractive enough to seek an opportunity elsewhere. An opportunity that immediately starts with a training contract.

Coincidentally, a previous solicitor in my team has moved on to another firm that has given her an opportunity to work part time, in line with her child career arrangements. She has previously asked if I wanted to continue as a caseworker at her current firm. I denied her previously as I was under the illusion that I would secure a training contract here.

But now the situation has changed and I needed to adapt. I call her and discuss with her at length whether a genuine training contract opportunity is available – one that is ready and written in writing. She explained that she will speak to the founding partner at her firm and they will get back to me.

Sure enough, I get a call directly from the founding partner. It is not like the behemoth of a place that I was currently at. It was a much smaller outfit, and had one solicitor who regularly featured in legal journals and commendations, repeatedly being described as "extremely dedicated" and the "legal Queen".

A day and time is set for an interview, sometime after 6pm.

I turn up at the office which is only a stone's throw from my 4 x 4m prison cell, masquerading as my flat (the perks of living in London).

I enter and a polite but extremely old receptionist greets me. There is an air of vampire, skulls and coffins to the place. I am told to sign in on an eroding notebook. An old printer sits behind her, ejecting paper after paper and then abruptly jamming. The reception area is a dying beige with various dying pot plants and the smallest Christmas tree I have ever seen – no larger than a desk fan.

Sandra, the founding partner, hobbles in and greets me with a raspy voice and a thick cigarette stench. She takes me up to her fourth floor office (via the stairs) which is adorned with various gothic pictures of Christ and Roman Catholic Christian memorabilia.

We jump right in to the conversation and it was informal from start to end. I tried throwing in some key facts about myself, that I technically run cases and barely need any supervision, generate money and work solo and in a team, but just need a damn training contract! But for each line of questioning, Sandra dwindles off on a tangent about how many ethnics live in the area now which was once upon a time a thriving town for hardworking English and Polish folk that fought in the war.

I decide to entertain her weird conversation style and begin talking about the history of the town, explaining that I was raised her for many many years. I can see immediately that she was taking a liking to me. She calls up what she referred to as her "right hand female general".

A mid-thirties, tall, muscular blonde-haired woman appears in the room dressed in casual gym clothing. She immediately asks how much I expect to earn working here. I think for a moment. I am currently on 18,000. Following the 3,000 accreditation "bonus" increase from 15,000. Let me add a further 4,000 just to test the water.

"22,000 at least and a training contract. I am ready to begin my period of recognised training as soon as possible."

"Done, Amir. I will draw up a contract confirming a training contract to start immediately upon six months of probation."

I stop her in her tracks.

"Six months won't do. Thank you for the opportunity but I will pass."

"Fine, three months. It is simply a formality. Any place you go to has to have some form of probation period just to ease you in!" Sandra laughs and coughs a large amount of phlegm into a bloody tissue.

The right hand woman sticks out a hand to shake. The tip of her fingernails dark blue with dirt and what I can only describe as possible orange earwax.

I hesitate for a moment.

"Sorry what is your name?"

"My name is Ellga Moriovic. I am a solicitor and advocate here."

"And she dated my son, too" Sandra nudges her with her elbow and winks. They begin to laugh and slap each other on the back.

I interrupt their moment.

"22,000 and a guaranteed, and I mean guaranteed, training contract upon completion of three months probation period."

Yes, they chime together.

"Our current trainee is completing her contract this month. You fit in as next in line as our trainee!"

I shake their hands and leave the building. I receive the draft contract via email as I arrive to my flat. I sit down and read it.

"2.1.2 The Firm will guarantee the Employee (you) a training contract to commence immediately upon acceptable completion of a preliminary three month probation period."

"2.1.3 The Firm will further train the Employee in Advocacy, and will pay all fees to ensure you obtain Higher Rights of Audience in the Civil Courts."

Wow. That bonus I did not expect.

I read the contract twice. It appeared to say exactly what I wanted it to say. But certain words started fogging my thoughts. "Acceptable completion"... why not just say completion. Preliminary ... three month probation period ... why not just three month probation period. I am no contract lawyer but this particular contract started to not fill me with the confidence that I needed.

I call up the friend at this firm. I ask her if they ever fired anyone or made issues with the current trainee there. She explains that she has only been there for nine months but no issue has propped up on her end. She explained that the three other solicitors at the firm were pleasant.

I call up my supervisor. I tell him that I am thinking of leaving. He explained that he feels hurt on my behalf and understands my reasoning for wanting to leave. I read out the passages of the draft contract and ask about his opinion. He explains that his contract once upon a time was worded in a similar way.

I sleep on it and wake up. Let me allow Yennifa an opportunity to salvage something.

5. Jumping Ship

Every Monday at around 10:00am, Yennifa walks in and demands we congregate in a meetings room to discuss our targets. There, she is provided by someone upstairs a breakdown of all our billable hours and what percent we have hit for each day in the last week.

I decide that this may be my best opportunity to corner Yennifa one-on-one, where if she decides to kick up a fuss, there wouldn't be the eyes and ears of everyone on our floor enjoying the spectacle. As expected, Yennifa runs down the list of "underperformers", which consist of about the entire team, and the "Golden children", which to be specific is actually a Golden Child – the now trainee solicitor who was assisted in the accreditation exam. Yennifa repeatedly mentioned that the Golden Child's mother was an alcoholic, and Yennifa, being the saviour that she is, thought of saving.

"Amir – you're on 88%. Get the 12% by the end of the week. I will check it again on Friday evening."

"John – you've billed three times your salary, but your billable hours have dipped. This is unacceptable regardless of how smart you think you are. Work on it."

"Christine – I will have to refer you to another team on the floor. I don't think you're cut out for our work. Please do not take it personally. 75% of your billing target can be hit by me on a bad day in less than six hours."

"Golden Child – well done on your work recently! I have had a read of your representations and this is exactly the lawyer I want you to be – firm but kind! Keep it up."

The episode went on and Yennifa dismissed the team, wasting 20 minutes of our time which could have been used to work on those never-ending billable targets. Regardless, I saw her move towards the exit and I ask if I can have a private word.

She stares and maintains her eye contact with me as she slowly reverses back in to her seat. Her eyes ice blue. I break the ice forming around us immediately.

"Yennifa, this is regarding my training contract."

"For God's sake, Amir! You're really incessant", she cuts me off.

I fire back demanding that she lets me speak.

"I have been here for two years now, Yennifa. I am accredited, I have billed atleast twice my salary. I rarely take sick days, and I am here grinding day in and day out. I have completed my law degree and the Legal Practice Course. I speak two languages which I use to the benefit of this company. All I ask is from you is to fight to get me a training contract."

Yennifa reaches into her backpack and pulls out my hours, with certain days circled in red.

"Here, on Monday last week you fall below 100% billable hours for the day, same with Thursday, this week. Here as well four weeks ago on a Wednesday you went down to 89%."

I lose my cool and ask her to compare me to her Golden Child in the team – like for like. Trainee Solicitor vs Caseworker, billable hour for billable hour. I start pointing at the hours of her Golden Child, of the hours of the other solicitors in the team. My hours are evidently ahead of her Golden Child, roughly on par with at least 4 out of 7 solicitors she had on the team. I point them out, they were there in black and white on her own little scoreboard.

"Well… what I can say is if you keep it up you will be a better solicitor than the Golden Child. However, I can't go to the man upstairs and show him your hours. He will never accept. Trust me on this Amir. I am actually looking out for you – saving you the embarrassment."

I sink into my chair. I feel like I am banging at a door that has been shut and now bolted.

"Fine. I hand in my resignation as of today. My contract dictates a one month notice period, and the clock begins now."

This was the first moment Yennifa took full notice of me. Her eyes were moving left and right as she tries to compute the situation. She quickly gets up and tells me to withdraw my notice and that she will deal with it.

She leaves the room and I follow her back to the floor. The keyboard banging, the mouse clicking and the telephone shouting continued to rage while my professional life was in pause. The world moves on with or without me, I thought.

Yennifa picks up a call and talks to the man upstairs.

I get an email from HR I would say within two minutes flat.

"Hi Amir, we offer you an unconditional training contract commencing immediately. Any further seats (departments) of your training are down to you."

I laugh to myself. All the late nights, all the driving down to prisons, mental health facilities, immigration removal centres, and nothing was noticed. I hand in my notice and now a red carpet is being rolled out for me.

Anger blurred my vision, red was all I can see. I reply declining the training contract and formally put my notice of resignation in writing.

Two banks down, I hear Yennifa shout the F word at her PC. The time strikes 6pm. I leave on time for the first time in two months. Yennifa retaliates by kicking me out of the Whatsapp work group as I leave and blocks my number.

6. New Start MkII

I commenced my role as a possible-trainee-but-first-need-to-complete-probation trainee at the start of 2018. I was given my own office on the ground floor with the ageing receptionist. I say office, more like an extension into Dracula's garden. I sit down and try to familiarise myself in my new surroundings. My former friendly colleague and now current colleague had her office also on the ground floor in another small and boxy extension into the garden. The office space is built like a Jenga set, with offices on top of each other, but separate to one and other. On each floor, separate offices with closed doors housed one or two solicitors. The place was tight but at the same time detached. My friendly colleague only worked two days a week and came in unusual hours of the day to fit around her child care arrangements.

She tells me that she is still in a probation period as hers is nine month due to her "part-time" status.

The receptionist walks me into each office space housing a solicitor or caseworker. She introduces me in an awkward break-in fashion. She would barge in with no knock, declare me as the latest addition, then proceed to slam the door shut. An interesting introduction. She then tells me that she remembers Sandra as a child. This confused me as Sandra looked almost as old as the receptionist. Then she tells me "I am her aunt actually". Well that explains it.

I am then lead to the locked room of my now new supervisor. The receptionist struggles to burst in as she realises midway that the room is locked. He then opens the door after a few embarrassing seconds of struggling. He introduces himself in a whisper as Peter Peeley. He then apologises, locks the door again, and evidently seems to be engrossed in some work.

The next solicitor to be rolled out to me was the Legal Queen, that is Dafna Blau. She had won various legal awards previously and her room was a maze of files and awards. She happily gets up from her chair and greets me heartily. She proceeds to take out a file list which I will inherit from a previous caseworker that left the firm recently due to a bereavement.

I see the list and it appeared to go on for pages, all stapled together. The growing cynic inside me is slowly connecting the dots. I am evidently needed to fill in for someone else's caseload.

Finally, I am taken to the top floor housing Sandra and Ellga, along with Ellga's assistant. Sandra, I am told by the receptionist only visits the office once every month or two following the brutal murder of her adult child. That shocks me, and my judgement of Sandra is suddenly called in to question in the trial that was going on in my mind. However, before I can ask any questions, the receptionist bursts in to the office of Ellga.

Ellga gets up from her cluttered desk in a low-ceiling attic office, wearing very high heels, a short office skirt but a sports lycra shirt, in an eye-watering non-sensical clash of gym casual and smart. She stubs out a cigarette, waves away the smoke cloud, and shakes my hand enthusiastically. She tells me that the probation period will be over like a flash and she is so happy to have me on board.

After some small talk, I return to my boxy office and see a copy of the new case list I have been given and over 75 files being aggressively arranged in my cabinet and slammed shut, drawer and drawer. I briefly peak into a handful of files and each one read as urgent. Court deadlines by tomorrow, court directions failed to be met by the previous fee earner, public authorities chasing the firm, experts threatening with action, complaints from clients, and outstanding counsel and expert fees unpaid for months. I am evidently going to be made to sweat over this three-month probation period before I get to the promised land. But I got the jist of the deal – they wanted these erupting cases to be dealt with, and I wanted a training contract. The game is the game, and again, I must play ball.

I began my endeavour to get on top of the caseload by trying to implement to arrange my work into reasonable chunks of urgent but not important, important but not urgent, urgent and important, and not important and not urgent files, utilising the method employed in a famous book written by Stephen Covey in his book The 7 Habits of Highly Effective People. To begin with, I would say it worked, but ultimately I could not keep up with it by the end.

I was driving through query after query, expediting cases, resolving outstanding fees, and meeting the deadlines set by various levels of the courts. I began to get a feel for my new caseload and was beginning to build rapport with some. To do so meant that I had to work beyond 8pm and stay on a bit longer to iron out more of the rough edges.

I would have to attend with minors to various interviews in Croydon then return to the office to begin work and preparation on next days batch of interviews, representations, and instructions to expert. I would see Dafna in the kitchen downstairs preparing her dinner. A jacket potato with cheese melted in the middle. She passes me by the door and tries to make conversation. I entertain her with a fake laugh and plenty of canine teeth visible and make my way to my office.

I begin again, day after day, night after night, a routine of travelling to either a detention centre, a prison, or an interviewing centre, then making it down to the office.

The firm demands that I sign in in a book every time we leave and every time we come back. I start to realise the timings of the other solicitors, trainees and admin in the office. The receptionist is consistent, she is here at 9am and out of office by 5:30pm. The current trainee is here by 8:30am and usually out by 8:00pm. But one of the numbers I see gets my attention from the corner of my eye. In at 9:00am, out by 4:00am? Surely that's a typo. I flick through the book and it's roughly the same times every day. In by 9:30am, out by 5:00am. In by 10:00am, out by 4:30am. In on Saturday and Sunday, 9 am to 9pm. Who is this machine of a human?! I look at the name and it is Dafna. I let out a gasp as my brain rattles to understand these times. Is she working almost every day to the early hours of the morning? Who does she owe money to? Loan sharks, surely! She is not a director, or the CEO. She is a salaried solicitor supervising a team of exactly one trainee solicitor.

I decide to query the insanity I saw on the register with my colleague, Sarah, who confirms the veracity of it all.

"Yes, she is a workaholic. I don't know why she does it though, so do not ask me again." I don't take her word for it. I approach the receptionist the next day while she is preparing her pale, lukewarm mug of tea in the basement kitchen.

"Hi, how was your evening last night?" I say politely, thinking she knew I was making my way down to the kitchen.

She lets out a muffled scream and tells me off. "Don't ever sneak up on me like that!" I apologise but was not going to let my curiosity go unanswered.

"Yes, Dafna is a powerhouse. She works those hours you mentioned. You should look up to her as an aspiring solicitor, Mr. Amir." She walks out of the kitchen and slams the door shut.

Firstly, I didn't like her referral to me as Mr. Amir. Secondly, is it even possible to top those hours? I would probably have to give up the luxury of sleep entirely.

I return to my desk and follow my own intuition and work in the current format I set up to get to the bottom of the 75 file allocation I was dealing with. I see the trainee solicitor in the garden which can only be accessed through my room. She is smoking. I haven't seen her smoke before. She looks at me and gives me a loose-handed wave, stubs out the cigarette, and begins drawing on another freshly lit cigarette.

I get an email from Ellga and it has the words 'urgent' in the topic line. I quickly open the door and read the longwinded and confusingly structured wording of the paragraphs she has typed. The email demands that I abide by my contract of billing three times my salary on a monthly basis. Various parts of the contract are quoted in a very legalese fashion, with constant mention of "with reference to paragraph... with reference to paragraph... you must do this. You should have billed this." The crux of the mumbled email was essentially stating that a month has elapsed and I have not provided the billing department (of one man, who by the way is the nephew of the Sandra) with enough files to amount to three times my monthly gross salary. I scratched my head. Yes, the contract did state this, but did they actually believe it can be done immediately, one month in, with barely enough time to review 75 cases, let alone decide if they can be billed? The email certainly did. I replied stating that I am not sure what the expectations are, but a period of one month is not enough to allow me to build my caseload, finalise them, get a decision, and bill. Roughly two minutes after I hit send, I get an email from Ellga, with paragraphs on paragraphs in it, making it look more like a novella then an email. She has cc'ed the CEO as well as my supervisor who I have yet to meet again physically (we did email) following the first day SWAT-style introduction led by Sandra the receptionist.

I decide to ignore the email and walk up to her attic office and iron out the confusion, and not allow email coldness and directness dictate what should be a relatively calm request. I knock on the door and she shouts me in. I walk in and I can barely see her from the cloud of what is now smoke from an e-cig.

"I am trying to cut out smoking real cigarettes, as you can see, so I've resorted to fake cigarettes", Ellga jokes.

She beckons me to sit down on a broken chair with no back support next to her. Her leg is shaking violently under the desk and her face is twitching.

"Amir, I did not mean to scare you with my email. I am just reminding you about your probation period and the need to satisfy our simple requirements. You do understand that we are a smaller business than your previous employer. We need to work a little harder, a little faster, and not waste time talking to the receptionist about Dafna."

"I understand that, and I am trying to sort out the files I have been given. But I am not sure how you expect me to already bill three times my salary in the first month", I reply dumbfounded.

"Bill the files of the previous fee earner that you have and we might allocate some of it to you. Also, you have to take on more cases unfortunately. The trainee solicitor here has a caseload twice as yours you know!"

So that is exactly what I ended up doing. I went down, identified files from the previous fee earner that can now be billed or stage billed (files that are not quite finished, but the Legal Aid Agency allows them to be billed up to the current stage), as well as chase private clients for outstanding money owed to the firm.

I triumphantly add all the incoming monies and according to my calculator, I should hit my billing target for the month, the grass should be green, and water should be wet. I email Ellga and the billing manager highlighting the files needing billing, send it off and get to work in my long sequence of attendances I have with worried clients.

Another email. I wonder from who? Ellga has returned bearing gifts. I open her gift and it's a glittering pile of… bad news.

"Dear Amir, clearly you haven't read your contract properly. If you go to section 10.8.1, it is clearly written that you are only entitled to a 10% uplift of billing allocated to you if you bill another colleague's file. Two times your salary is not enough. As such, you have not hit your monthly billing target. To be quite honest, I do not believe you are on track to hitting your target next month. I suggest an urgent meeting tomorrow morning with your supervisor. See you tomorrow at 9am sharp."

That night I struggled to sleep and when I did, it was a struggle. Numbers were haunting me. Nightmares were forming, led by The Count from Sesame Street and Ellga, singing along to "One and One Make Two times your salary is not enough!" I wake up with sweat soaking my shirt. I reign in my panic and remind myself that I have only been there at Slaviceks for one month. Ellga might just be a pedantic senior colleague, and surely someone else more senior will see sense.

I turn up to the 9am meeting sharp. I sit there and my supervisor comes in looking down at the floor. He whispers something but I could not make it out. Something about 'the morning'. Ellga waltz in with her face bright Donald Trump orange, lipstick smeared on her lips covering atleast a country mile north of her top lip. For a second I forget the purpose of the meeting and feel like breaking out into a laugh, then remember that I've essentially been called up for a disciplinary one month in!

Ellga sits down and just lets rip into my supervisor.

"You have not supervised him properly. That is why he thinks he can slack. I expect both of you to pick up your weights. This firm doesn't run on charity. We are a business!"

My supervisor attempted for a second to break the tirade, but quickly shriveled back and began nodding away like the Churchill dog.

I interrupt and attempt to explain the lunacy of the situation.

"Respectfully, Ellga, please listen. I have just joined a month ago. I have been shuttling between office to prison to detention centre the entire month whilst plowing through 75 files and ensuring they are up to speed. Every complaint I have dealt with, every file has been reviewed and ultimately corrected, and every client is now happy as far as I am aware. Can you please just give me time to settle in and I am sure the actual billing will come through. Please just look at my work in progress and that can show you the substantial work I have done to date."

"Yes, please do look at it. It is fine to me", my supervisor squeaks before looking down at his shoes again.

Ellga crossed her arms before softening up.

"The firm agrees. As such, the firm will allow you to proceed. The firm appreciates your work. Also, the firm will like to invite you to a training session."

I thank her for her time and got out of the room, agreeing to any training session she, sorry I mean "the firm", intends to send me to.

The training session actually turned out to be an internal session led by Ellga herself. Myself, my supervisor, the trainee, the receptionist, two solicitors, essentially 95% of the business apart from my colleague Sarah and the Sandra herself, attended. Ellga brought in her own laser pointer and also invited a barrister from a chambers that deals with a lot of the firm's appeal matters all the way up to the Supreme Court. Dafna sat there with her arms crossed as she eyed up Ellga prancing up and down the room whilst training us about "deportations from the UK and the rules". Ellga repeatedly cracked what appeared to be internal jokes with the barrister, which no one in the room apart from them understood. Dafna began correcting Ellga's blindingly obvious legal mistakes and inaccuracies. Ellga started off by ignoring Dafna and attempting to string sentences utilising as much of the thesaurus as she possibly can, sounding like a student desperately trying to bloat the word limit on a dissertation she knows she is failing in.

Dafna increased the intensity to the point it became obvious to all of us that Ellga did not really have a clue about immigration in general, or deportation in particular. Ellga then abruptly stormed out of the room, leaving us all shocked and confused. Dafna then stood up and continued the training session herself, barely able to hold back a curled smile throughout and giggling to herself every few minutes. The rest of us watched this spectacle as our lunch break vanished and Dafna demonstrated that she knew too much about immigration in general, and deportation in particular. The barrister explained that he had something urgent to attend to and haphazardly made his way out.

For the second month at Slavicek, I intended to bolster my position by demonstrating to the firm that despite still waiting for tens of decisions and court determinations to come through to allow me to bill files, I do enough work that once billed would actually provide more than three times my salary. I accepted as many new cases as possible, diverting most new queries to myself. I would work intensely on every file and by month's end, I had generated enough WIP (work in progress) that if billed, would generate 4 to 5 times my monthly salary for a month. I explained it all in an email to Ellga and expected an immediate seven-page reply, but to my surprise, no response came in. I told myself that no news is good news, and headed into month three of what was intended as a "short probationary period", but now is a trial by burnout.

As the days fizzed by, my curiosity of Dafna intensified and I began to periodically check in the register to see if she is keeping up with her insane hours. I drop the details of my investigation into this phenomenon to one of my close friends and his first response was, "Bro, there is no way on God's green Earth she is doing those hours. She's just pulling these times out of thin air (maybe 'thin air' was not the exact wording he used) as she leaves after everyone else."

I decide to test the theory. On a Saturday whilst on my latest ever trip to the gym at around one in the morning, I stopped by at the office. All the lights are on. I walk in and see Dafna crouched over her chair typing away at her desk and her printer singing away behind her. She has two whiteboards in her room with various caselaw names and numbers scribbled on them in a blur of writing. She had folders and books all around her like electrons circulating the nucleus that is Dafna. Also scattered around her were half-eaten jacket potato skins with mouldy looking cheese plates. She doesn't even realise I am there, and when she does raise her head to look at me, she is confused asking if I need help. I tell her I have forgotten something and make my way down. Does she even know what time it is? Why is she working so hard? I text my friend explaining that he should keep his conspiracies to himself. This Dafna is the real deal.

The next day an email is sent out explaining that when we approach the Christmas period, will be off during Christmas Day, Boxing Day and New Years but we all need to work in days between. Dafna replies to the email and copies in the entire firm, explaining that she is willing to come in and cover Christmas Day, Boxing Day and New Years, as well as the caseload of anyone that is not here during this festive period. She jokes at the end of her email that she doesn't "believe in the baby Jesus anyway".

Mid-December 2018

The CEO sends out a firm-wide email that she will be attending the office and will be ensuring and overseeing a "fair-distribution" of the caseload that has recently inundated the office. I was happy to hear this as I was looking at passing this probation period and beginning the training contract in a calmer fashion. She also mentions in her email that Dafna will be conducting the get-together, much to the fury of Ellga.

I can hear Ellga swan around the office on the morning of this meeting. She is slamming the printer shut, moving chairs that she believes are "misplaced", and arguing with the receptionist about the speed in which she types. The receptionist retorts "don't you have a meeting to set-up? Oh wait, you don't, so leave me alone."

The meeting convenes without the presence of the CEO to begin with. Dafna is sitting down and massaging as section of her stomach. Ellga is there looking a bright shade of orange and red. Myself and the trainee are there sat side-by-side, each holding a long list of current cases that we hope would be redistributed. My supervisor is sitting at a chair closest to the door. He gives me a nervous smile and looks back down at his shoes.

The CEO comes crashing in. Ellga runs over to grab her a chair. She sits her down next to her. She whispers angrily in her ear, and the CEO nods away like a thoughtful judge hearing the impact statement of a wronged victim.

Dafna begins by briefly going through our caseload. Ellga runs out and comes back with a sandwich for the CEO. The CEO whispers a joke in her ear. She whispers back. They cackle for what felt like an age.

I jump in and explain to Dafna that I have recently taken over a number of cases which I feel can be distributed as my current caseload has a significant amount of preparation needed to progress them over the coming month. Dafna cuts me off and beckons her trainee to speak first. The trainee airs the same grievance as me. Dafna pontificates for a moment before declaring:

"Hand them to Amir. Amir you will take on her recent caseload. Come and collect them from my room. Thank you."

I attempt to resist but Ellga loudly starts discussing Value Added Tax and its applicability to one of Dafna's cases.

"I have looked through this particular file, Dafna. You have not factored in VAT. As you should already know, a client with lawful residence or Temporary Admission to the UK should ordinarily be VAT claimable."

"I don't know what you're talking about Ellga", Dafna snorts as she nervously tries to laugh off this tangent conversation.

Ellga proceeds to pull out a blue folder from under her chair. She hands it over to the CEO.

"If you see here, Dafna has repeatedly not charged VAT on the file. As such, it will be coming out of your pocket."

The CEO's face turned sun-ripened tomato red and she ends the Amir-inherits-all-files session there and then.

We shuffle out of the room, and immediately as the door is shut, Dafna and Ellga are screaming at the top of their lungs at each other.

Later that day, I go up to Dafna's room to pick up my additional caseload. She has put her doctor on loudspeaker as she furiously types away. She points at a 5-foot pile of folders placed into a small trolley. I grab the trolley and make my way out of the room. As I am leaving, I can hear the doctor exclaim, "Dafna, you have to take it easy! Recent tests show your kidneys are struggling. I can sign you off work."

Dafna slams the phone shut.

As the evening went on and I spend time going through this new caseload, highlighting any impending deadlines, I get an email. It's from Ellga, and the environment was toxic so I knew that it cannot be good news.

The email reads as follows:

"Dear Amir, having explained to the CEO your inability to bill three times your salary, your probation period will be extended for an additional three months pending sufficient demonstration of your billing capabilities."

I fell back in my chair as it began to dawn on me the game Ellga was playing. This was no probation period. This was a ploy to get me to progress outstanding cases the firm did not want to handle, from the previous fee earner's caseload, to the current trainee's caseload. The carrot will be dangled in front of me and it was becoming increasingly apparent that no amount of hardwork and progress will change her mind.

I reply back demanding a meeting. Ellga tells me to come upstairs to her office. I go up and she is sitting at the CEO's desk looking out of the window, smiling to herself. The room is jampacked with crosses and pictures of the Virgin Mary. There is only one light and it is shining on Ellga's orange face.

I stumble to find a chair and sit down. I explain to her as diplomatically as I could, without breaking down in tears that I believe I should start my training contract, and the work in progress will come in naturally as decisions and determinations come in. I repeat the mantra I have been trying to explain to all my opportunity-denying seniors from the previous firm to this one: work in progress flows in! I felt a lump form in my throat as I contemplate if I will ever get this training contract.

Ellga resolutely stands up and exclaims "no billing, no contract."

She then pushes an addendum contract where it states that I agree that I will not qualify for a training contract unless I bill three times my salary on a monthly and rolling basis, as well as "satisfactorily get signed off by the CEO and those she has delegated, such as Ellga Marionovic." The thesaurus heavy and overly expressive style of drafting made it evidently clear that it is her drafting work.

I take the addendum contract and left the dark office with a head pounding to a painful migraine.

My time at Slaviceks was clearly a false flag, and I decided that I do not have the appetite to indefinitely wait for a moment of mercy from Ellga to bestow a training contract on to me.

The character of Ellga exists in numerous work places. They are senior colleagues who usually hold sway and authority over more junior workers, clash with actual senior workers like Dafna, and do not have a defined role themselves. They are "senior", but if I was to sit Ellga down to summarise her precise role, I can bet my bottom dollar she would not be able to. As such, to "fit in" and show her seniors, the CEO in this instance, that she is a valuable member of the organisation, she clashes with others, pretends to occupy a 'training and development' role for more junior colleagues, and generally throwing in barriers and arbitrary tasks to appear to have an actual job other than just a job title. For the younger readers of this book, beware of what the anthropologist David Graeber refers to in his book Bullshit Jobs as the 'Task-Masters' – who in my experience was Ellga Marionovic! They will not deliver you to the promised land – but they will certainly deliver heartache, long nights, awkward meetings and false dreams.

7. A Desperate Plea

I had a long heart-to-heart with a friend of a colleague who was looking to help his new firm recruit. He himself, let us call him Ranveer, has recently joined and was already being a pristine employee looking to help the new firm he was at. I explained the quagmire I was in. He was sympathetic and wanted me to get a training contract, aware of my previous travails at the large legal aid firm as told by my colleague to him. He told me to forward to him my CV and he will speak to one of the directors in the firm that he works under to try to persuade him to sign me up as trainee.

I received an email promptly from the director. He was actually a barrister but occupied the position of director in this firm. Let us call this firm Jobson Solicitors. In a simple one-liner, he asked me to meet him on a specific day, at a specific time, at the "City of London" office.

I turned up bang on time, despite doing laps around the maze that is the Bank central line station. I would like to meet the architect of that station in the afterlife, turn him into a mouse, and test experimental shampoo on his eyes.

Anyway, the office this firm occupies, was located in a very fancy and historic building quite close to the vicinity of the station. I have never seen a firm that does not specialise in corporate mergers and acquisition occupy an office in such a posh part of London. After slotting my jaw back in its place after it hit the floor, I went in and met the director. He was a burly man, towered over me, with his shirt buttons on the brink of detonation. I could hear them plea to me to move my head as they intended to eject out into orbit.

Surprisingly, he did not end up taking me to the office. Rather, he sat me down in a corridor table and chairs. I had my pitch ready and I was not going to sign up to his Jobson firm unless I start immediately as a trainee. No mirage "probation period". No review of my billing performance. Immediate Formula One style start, straight out of the hatch.

The pitch worked and the director, who a colleague later on in my time angrily referred to him as Mr. Krabs from Spongebob Square Pants, agreed to take me on immediately as a trainee solicitor.

I received the confirmation from the Solicitors Regulation Authority that my training contract has commenced and will last a period of two years.

Also received in the post was my contract. It was way less wordy than the one Ellga gave me, and very boilerplate and oven-ready. Typical terms and typical times.

A week before I was set to formally attend the office for my first day, I receive a call from Mr. Krabs' wife, who I learn to be the training principal. The training principal is the person in the firm designated to oversee the training of the trainee solicitors and to ultimately 'sign' them off at the end to confirm that they are ready to be admitted to the roll of solicitors.

She was very snappy and spoke at an outstanding speed.

"You're the fella starting in a week, right? Have you signed the contract? I am sending you an amended one. I'm not happy with the one sent to you. These terms in the new contract are in line with the trainees currently here."

I asked that it be forwarded to my email so that I can sign and return it.

When I receive it, it is almost identical to the one I already signed but with three key details. The first being that I must work additionally on Saturdays. The second is, instead of finishing at 6pm, it would be a 6:30pm finish. The third being, instead of working out of the City office, I will be working out of a new office that they have opened on a high street in North West London.

I attempt to call back the training principal, let's call her Big B. She does not pick up. I call her secretary who does pick up. He explains that Big B is extremely busy and will get back to me in due course. Days elapse and I start to worry. My expected start day is any day now and I did not want to mess up the start before I even walk through the door. More importantly, my wife was pregnant and was expected to give birth in the first half of my training contract. Saturdays will be days I can step in and help her soon-to-be ridiculous workload.

After sending out a number of emails, and finally resorting to cc'ing Mr. Krabs, she picked up one of my calls.

I explained my conundrum, my wife's pregnancy, and the original contract was already signed.

She snapped at me and said "okay, fine. We'll review it again in six months and that is non-negotiable." She then hangs up.

Despite the abruptness, I was happy with her response. Would she remember this conversation six months down the line? Probably not. Am I going to start my training contract finally? Absolutely!

8. You're dead to us now

February 2019

I drafted my resignation email to Slavicek and awaited a response. I expected alarm bells to go off. I expected Ellga, the CEO, and Dafna to turn on the bat signal. Who is going to inherit my newly opened files, my inherited files, and the files that have been redirected to me from the trainee solicitor there?

I receive a response immediately. It reads:

"That's a shame. Best of luck."

No exit interview. No request for renegotiations. Nothing at all. When I turned up on the final day after serving my one week notice period (the notice period put in by Ellga for those in a probation period), Ellga and Dafna seemed to have kissed and made up and walked into my office together. They both demand I prepare all files I have for a new fee earner to come in and take over.

I explain that many have recently been allocated to me by the trainee. Dafna puts both hands on my table, stares at me dead on in the space between my eyes and goes:

"Do you know how many times I bill of my salary? Four times. Four times, Amir! I pay for you and your salary!"

Ellga stands behind her sniggering, before leaving my room slowly.

A few minutes after, Ellga walks back in and seemed to finish off the threat Dafna lobbed my way.

"And if you don't, we can report you to the SRA for misconduct, so wherever you're going, it will follow you if you do not sort out the files."

The threat was real in my mind and, again, I did not want to sabotage the blessing of starting a training contract immediately at Jobson without an excruciating probation period.

I burnt the midnight oil as I ploughed through file after file, to ensure each one was up-to-date and ready for a handover. I checked funding forms, outstanding client fees, counsel fee notes, expert invoices, as well as the unimportant bits like properly progressing the legal case which no one seemed to care about yet in my short legal career! Each file was meticulously checked by Dafna before she agreed for it to be put in a handover pile – similar to the one that was dumped in my room when I joined. The clock struck 1am, the church next door bonged once to confirm this, and I was done. I shut the lights in my small boxy room for the final time – a room I will not occupy again. I thought to myself that a lot of stress, anxiety, and pain was felt in that room in such a short and intense space of time. I thanked God anyway and left the room. No one came down to say goodbye or wish me well. Dafna's lights were on upstairs, as well as her trainee. Maybe the trainee took the advice of the receptionist and is trying to mirror Dafna to become a legal somebody. I walked out into the cold and chilly London air, with my breath forming before me, creating ghostly-looking clouds of vapour. Breathe Amir, it is time to start your training contract.

9. Rat Race

March 2019

I opted to start almost immediately following a weekend that went by in a flash (mainly sleep and more sleep). I was desperate to commence and be in the training contract, as I would technically have enhanced employment protection as an 'apprentice'. To terminate my training contract would require the firm to go through the Solicitors Regulation Authority – the overseeing body that regulates all solicitors in England and Wales and admits them to the solicitors roll when a trainee is considered ready and has been 'signed off' by the firm's designated training principal. On the morning of my first day, I hit the ground running. I was allocated a supervisor. Let us anoint him with the name Ranveer. The office that I will be working from would be a new office that the firm has recently opened in the North West of London, imaginatively called the North West office, and intended to open them up to new business from that side of London. Jobsons also had offices on the high streets south of the river, and of course the City of London office, which Mr. Krabs was very proud of.

I took the bus to the office on my first day, dressed in a now brand new grey suit, pinstripes this time. No more baggy suits – this was slim and tapered in all the right places. I gave the estate agents a run for their money. I even dug up one of my wrist watches to look the part, and those tie clips that stop the tie flapping on your face on a windy day.

As I got off the bus to attend the office on my first day, I was greeted with a stench of burnt fast food oils and flies hovering over littered half-empty burger boxes and spilt drinks. A man with barely any clothes on was pushed out of the betting shops down the road. He began running towards me.

"Spare a change mate? Spare a change fella?" he shouted as snot dribbled out of his nostrils akimbo.

I politely decline and walk towards the office with quicker and longer strides. I hear some profanities I assume are directed towards me before it got drowned out by the beeping of car horns, the sound of reversing trucks and lorries, and the grunting noise of hundreds of people on the streets going about their business.

The office was located above a fabric store, and next door to another law firm. I looked down and as far as the eye can see, it was a swarm of fast food shops, betting shops, high street law firms, barbers, and stands selling sweetcorn and mangoes (in winter? What sort of sorcery). There was no lift as the steep stairs led up to a single door. I go in and there is no receptionist and no one to greet me. I make a coughing noise and my old colleague Ranveer springs out behind one of the office rooms. He is ecstatic seeing me, and I was happy to see him and grateful for his referral that essentially got me here.

He showed me around and the office, and it was larger than that of Slaviceks. Each fee earner had a room surprisingly, and they were all near each other. There was a kitchen with a working light and toilets with a working flush. All I needed was silver kitchenware.

I was shown to my room and it was relatively spacious. The office did have a seventies vibe, with grey ceilings, fluorescent lights, wooden flooring and brown wooden walls. I sat down on my desk which had no computer or telephone linked up. I asked Ranveer and he explained that he had to wait weeks before they brought it down. He allowed me to use a laptop which I wasn't sure was the firm's or his. General Data Protection Regulation (GDPR) went straight out of the window but I did not mind. I called Big B's admin and he did not pick up my calls so I accepted the temporary solution and Ranveer dug up an old telephone from the storage room, which, after inhaling dust particles from the Cold War era and causing me a cough that punished my lungs for the entire day, it worked!

Now, what else do I need? It hit me. I don't have an office chair. Ranveer, all giddy and excited was running from room to room trying to find me a chair. They were all broken in different ways. One did not have a backrest, another had squeaky and disjointed wheels, and a third was permanently in an elevated position. I opted for the one permanently in an elevated position. At the very least, it would give me gravitas as clients walked into my office. I had to thank J Edgar Hoover for that tip.

Ranveer, with a smile now covering the surface area of his entire lower half of his face, remembered the name of my wife and asked about her. I explained that she is pregnant and soon I will be off for paternity leave. Ranveer let out a happy scream. He began asking about my wife's "nesting" ritual. I had no idea what he was talking about. I asked him about my new colleagues. He showed me to two other rooms where a solicitor sat working away, and a corner office housing the other trainee.

Ranveer explained that now we are a complete team, with two solicitors and two trainees.

I asked about Mr. Krabs, Big B and the other directors of the firm, and whether they attend. Ranveer explained that they generally do not and rely on us to run this new branch of the firm. He explained that one of the directors is Mr. Krabs brother, called Nemo. Mr. Krabs was head of public law. Mr. Krabs wife, Big B, was head of family law, and the training principal who will confirm and sign off my training contract at the end. Nemo was head of immigration. Mr. Krabs and Nemo's nephew was head of crime. He leaned over and whispered, "I am the de facto office coordinator here too! A solicitor and an office coordinator!" I was impressed with the trust seemingly put in the most excitable man alive, with no receptionist, no paralegal, and generally no visits.

I asked about Mr. Jobson himself. Where does he fit in?

"Oh, don't you know? He essentially retired a long time ago and the firm is run and owned by Mr. Krabs and his family. Mr. Krabs said having Jobson's caucasian-sounding name on the door helps drive clients in. He is so business-savvy. I love it!"

Not how I would describe it, but business is business I guess.

My eyes were searching for the pile of files I will inherit. I was prepared for the tsunami-high wave that was going to pound on me any second now.

"So, Ranveer. Where are my clients' files."

He pointed at three cabinet drawers with four individual drawers in each. I opened them and each drawer was filled to the brim with files packed with serious looking papers, with the logos of Her Majesty's Courts and Tribunals Service, Home Office, and Government Legal Department emblazed on many.

"How many are there?!", I panicked.

"Oh, only 145 files. The other trainee is on 230 files at the moment", he whispered in a sudden serious tone before returning to a beaming smile.

As insane as that number is, at least I am in my training contract, I told myself. It is a fixed term contract lasting exactly two years. This time in two years, I will be signed off by Big B who is the training principal, admitted to the roll of solicitors by the SRA, and the world will be my oyster. Patience is the name of the game. All I needed was patience.

I began looking at the files and two thirds had the exact same surname. I joked about how they are all related. I looked at some of their asylum claims and they were almost carbon copies of each other.

July 2019

The months rolled on and I worked robotically to progress my caseload. Not to toot my own horn too much, but I truly was approaching a level of independence and efficiency in my work from all the difficult experiences I encountered, that I can roll over cases in a timed and professional manner.

As for this firm, in contrast to the other firms I worked in, they had interpreters, experts, friends, and connections to Mr. Krabs and his family that bring the cases to fee earners directly. The firm had an 'always say yes' attitude, which might sound inspirational and hard-working, but in reality meant that we had to deal with every single case coming through the door. When you're knee-deep in over 140 active cases, the phone is ringing off the hook on the minute with anxious clients calling for the umpteenth time to seek "updates" which were provided to them in the last working day, and clients being waved straight into your room (direct orders from Mr. Krabs and Nemo). The say yes attitude quickly spirals into something of abuse towards the fee earner.

A while into my training contract, Nemo suddenly began attending the office more regularly. The office went from one extreme to the other, barren with not a single overseeing senior figure from the management present, to an all present Nemo. Mr. Krabs remained in the fancy City office, whilst Big B remained in the South East England offices.

We would hear Nemo's various 4x4s roar near the entrance, which myself and the other trainee began to become familiar with. Sometimes it was a Range Rover, other times it was a Porsche Cayenne, and finally an Audi Q8. He would have his car keys in a jangly chain that he would spin on his index finger as he comes up the stairs. Interestingly, despite being a middle-aged man with a gut invading the entire circumference of his waist and belt, he would run up the stairs. It appeared to me to be eccentric behaviour that was ultimately harmless. However, as I found out later on, it was intended to "catch" us acting up or not working hard enough.

As Nemo's attendances ramped up in the office, emails began popping up in our inbox coinciding with his recent visits from Nemo's brother, Mr. Krabs, titled, "Recent observations".

"Dear West/North West London Office,

It come to my atencion, that people not wearing ties in office. And shoes have dirt on them. This is very unprofessional. We are lawyers, not grocery green sellers. Fix this.

Thanks.

Mr. Krabs (okay, he doesn't sign it off as Mr. Krabs) – Barrister (yes, he signed off his emails with his occupation like we somehow forgot. And no, it is not his saved signature as he would email from his iPhone and sometimes even misspell his beloved "barrister" occupation)."

I look down at my smart and ironed shirt with blazer and realise that I forgot to wear a tie. Oh well. I'll bring it in tomorrow. Not sure why a smart, ironed office shirt, with a blazer and suit trousers is not sufficient in the middle of the concrete jungle we were working out from, but hey ho.

Moments later, Ranveer comes flying in to my room in a blind panic. I stand up thinking he has a medical issue as he is panting and beads of sweat are dripping off his forehead.

"Have you seen the email?! They're referring to me!", he bellows.

He sticks out his shoe and there is mud caked around the sole.

"I hope I do not get the sack! I walked through the park with my office shoes. Oh no!"

I calmed Ranveer down, tried my best in explaining to him that it is nothing to be worried about, and returned to my desk. During the period of calming Ranveer and returning to my chair, my phone rang five times from various clients. I desperately tried to call back as I knew the policy of this firm involves being ever-present and available for all clients and potential clients. However, I was too late. The calls were rerouted to reception, the receptionist (as directed by Big B emailed me requesting an explanation, copying in Big B, Mr. Krabs and Nemo.

I reply with a lie explaining that I was discussing a legal matter with my supervisor, Ranveer, briefly in his room. Seconds later, Big B has copied in Ranveer asking why I was not available to pick up the calls that came to my phone. I urged Ranveer to go with my white lie. Ranveer does not, and replies nervously that I was talking to him at the door of my room regarding Mr. Krabs latest email.

We both get an email bollocking. I serve my own separate bollocking to Ranveer.

"Are you thick, Ranveer?! You know how they are! Why would you compromise us both?", I spit angrily at him.

"But we can't lie. I don't know. I feel uncomfortable lying. Sorry", he said looking down at his shoes.

I feel like a father telling off his unruly son, yet he was eleven years older than me, entering his forties. Should I be speaking to a grown adult like this, I began asking myself?

We worked the rest of the day in silence.

End of July 2019

The phone is ringing at 8am. I have just arrived in the office. It is Nemo.

"Hello, I will visit the office tonight. How much are you billing this month?"

"Around 4900GBP. It will be ready for you by the end of the day, hopefully", I reply in my most cheerful voice.

"That is below 5000GBP. This is not three times your salary", Nemo's voice turns.

"I have been here less than six months, Nemo. How do you-"

"I am a director in this firm and you are just a trainee! I have been a solicitor for over thirty years – before you were even born! How dare you reply like that to me?! I can revoke your training contract just like that – I have done it before. Say okay and move on!", his voice crackles down the phone. I am unsure how to reply, so sheepishly follow his veiled threat and say okay and proceed to hang up.

Nemo then follows up a call on the hour every hour until 6pm.

"Hello, is the billing ready?"

I finally prepare the files and send it through electronically to the billing manager. I call the billing manager to confirm if everything is in order and can hear Nemo and Mr. Krabs in the background.

"Check every page of his file. Check it, check it, check it. We can't lose a penny of it. This is business", Mr. Krabs says.

"I put him in his place, don't worry", Nemo replies to Mr. Krabs.

I repeat my question to the billing manager whose voice sounds like she has just cried and is now trying to maintain her composure.

"Yes, Amir. All is good. We are billing your files tonight."

I throw myself into my chair and breathe a loud sigh of relief. My moment of relief is immediately interrupted when my phone lights up again.

'Nemo' reads on the telephone. I pick up.

"Hi Amir, what do you anticipate to bill for the coming month of August?"

Now, patience and professionalism are all fine and dandy when you are dealing with someone that has a modicum of understanding and professionalism to begin with. But it became blatantly obvious that I am not dealing with a person of understanding and professionalism. At that moment, I lose my composure.

"You are unbelievable, Nemo! How dare you harass me like this over billing? I just provided you with my files for this month after over ten calls from you throughout the day! I have been here for less than six months and I have already provided the firm with my entire salary in billings, and I have inherited three senior fee earners caseload!"

"What did you just-"

Suddenly, Nemo's voice is interrupted and another different yet equally as nasal voice appears on the line.

"Hi, Mr. Krabs the barrister here. No problem, Amir. Have good night", Mr. Krabs says, and the line disconnects.

Ranveer appears near my door looking at me with his child-like eyes through the crack of the hinges.

"You should not speak to the senior directors like that, Amir. You might get fired", he says sullenly.

I ignore Ranveer, shut the lights to my office and walk out without saying a word. My ears feel like they have caught fire. I am fuming. I stop at the bus stop and there is a delay of over twenty minutes. I decide to walk it home. One hour and a half later, I am at the door to my flat – knees in pain from all the walking but still fuming! The bus I was supposed to board just passes by. I would take that as a victory in a day of losses.

August 2019

Another email hits my mailbox from the firm directors, Mr. Krabs, Big B, and Nemo. It concerns, you guessed it, billing!

Dear Amir

You are now expected to hit 3.5 times your salary, rather than the three you were previously contractually obligated to hit. This is because you are a trainee solicitor, and 3 times salary will be reserved for paralegals who are less experienced.

Your contract will be modified to reflect this.

If you do not hit your targets, as per our usual procedure, you will be warned. If no improvements are made, this will escalate, and can likely cause you to be let go.

Please do not hesitate to contact us for any further queries.

Big B on behalf of Management

I was not aware that a contract could be modified unilaterally without any input or negotiation from the other side. I was not completely sure, as a trainee solicitor, that I actually had concrete billing targets like this, and can essentially be punished for not meeting them. A "period of recognised training" yet being penalised for not making the firm money. Very intriguing. So intriguing I decided to follow up and not "hesitate" to contact them.

I attempted to call the training principal and director, Big B. No answer. I leave a voicemail and follow up with an email.

The trot of Nemo is heard as he gallops up the stairs, arriving at the reception area and office rooms shouting and berating us.

"Why are not ALL the lights on downstairs?! This is a business and you are all playing games with us! We pay you salaries for what exactly?" he froths, as white spit gelatinises around the edges of his lips, and glides metres to hit me in the face.

I interrupt his tirade and ask him if he can clarify the latest email about the changes in billing targets.

"You are a trainee solicitor. When I was your age, I was working a minimum of 12 hours a day. I have looked at your hours. Dave from the South East England office has billed more than you. He is also a trainee. Dig deep or leave."

"Sorry Nemo, I want to speak to Big B. She is my training principal and I have yet to even speak to her since joining, let alone see her", I shoot back.

Nemo picks up his phone. Nemo, hitting sixty or appearing to hit sixty, has named Big B, the young wife of his elderly brother Mr. Krabs, "Aunty" on his cracked screen iPhone 5. He goes to Ranveer's room and whispers into his phone. Thirty seconds later my phone rings. It's Big B herself.

"The billing target reflects the fact that we are a business and we have to pay many people's salaries including yours, notwithstanding rent and bills. Also, Serena, the litigation trainee in the City office, has billed more than you. So I can't see why you can't bill as much as her. Does that answer your questions? Can I return to my work? I am very busy", Big B splutters in one breath, with no introduction.

"But I did not know that trainees can be let go for not hitting their billing targets. I thought the Solicitors Regulation

Authority make clear that I am essentially an apprentice, and that I have rights-"

Before I can finish my sentence, just like Nemo, Big B loudly interrupts me.

"Listen here, I am an SRA-approved training principal. If you're not happy, I can terminate your training contract and you can continue your training elsewhere."

I have worked so hard to get here and had no intention to come to a point like this.

"Okay, I will try-"

Big B hangs up.

Nemo walks into my office seconds later with his hands in his pocket staring at me dead on.

"Are you satisfied, boy? You have chargeables to get. Do your work."

September 2019

As the legal representatives of some detained clients in various detention centres, we are legally entitled and obligated to attend their interviews with the Home Office, in the centres themselves.

The Home Office have a guidance on the immigrants that cannot be detained, or should be released if detained. They are generally potential/actual victims of trafficking, victims of torture who have not had their claims decided, severely ill individuals, pregnant women, and families. That is not to say the Home Office do not detain them. It is common practice for them to do so, and then face a firm lodging complicated, detailed and many-a-times urgent judicial review applications (a process challenging the lawfulness of a decision or process; not to be confused with an appeal) on behalf of these immigrants arguing unlawful detention, resulting in massive damages being paid out to various detainees, which is then spun by certain tabloid newspapers that immigrants are essentially scamming thousands from taxpayers money and "activist" lawyers that are stopping foreign criminals being sent 'home'.

I rock up tired and exhausted, leaving my home at 5am to make the three hour drive down to the detention centre, where my client is detained.

I am greeted with a detention officer who does not even work for the Home Office, rather a private company that runs the centre on behalf of the Home Office.

"Hi, I'm here for Mr. Nguyen's substantive interview", I say, happy that my mind is still operating on four hours of sleep.

"Yes, let me search you. Still not made enough money playing with people's lives and getting government money, have you?" she says out of the blue.

I am stunned and confused, and genuinely about to burst out laughing.

"I'll continue to get paid for as long as you continue to help detain them", I retort.

She grunts and tightly grips my forearm, tying my visitors tag around my wrist. My colleague will search you now as I have something else to do. She points at her six foot six tattoo'ed colleague who should be on stage at Mr. Olympia, rather than this deserted centre next to an airport.

After being roughly touched in every sensitive part of my body, I was allowed into the interview room. Mr. Nguyen was there patiently waiting, and by patiently waiting, I mean he was fast asleep.

I wake him up and he is happy to see me.

"Mr. Amir! Thank you! You are here! Thank you!", he screams at the top of his lungs.

The interviewing officer comes in with an interpreter that looks as sleepy as Mr. Nguyen.

The interviewing officer begins typing away at her laptop. She explains that she will ask him many questions about his asylum claim, and type them all up, and a copy will be given to him at the end of the day.

Mr. Nguyen nods aggressively in agreement.

Mr. Nguyen then does something that surprises us all. He begins removing his jumper. Followed by his jumper, he begins removing his trousers. Suddenly he was standing there stark naked.

The interviewing officer screams and recoils to press the emergency strip lined across the back of the room.

"I was tortured in Russia! Release me from detention!" Mr. Nguyen screeches.

I am frozen in my chair, half enjoying the spectacle, the other half confused as to what I should be doing as his legal representative.

Mr. Olympia comes crashing in with his sidekicks and they tackle, restrain and take Mr. Nguyen away.

I am shortly after also escorted out. But my route seemed to be straight for the exit. I am told the Home Office will shortly fax over a letter to us for a rescheduled interview.

I begin my journey back to London, with my eyes barely capable of maintaining eye contact with the car right in front of me. I come within inches of hitting the car in front, and on numerous occasions swerve dangerously close to the ramps on the far right side of the motorway. I get off at the next service station. I get a double shot espresso and red bull, and concoct a mixed cocktail of the two. Surely, this will wake me up. It did wake me up. I arrive in London in record time with my ears buzzing.

I arrive in the office and Nemo has two new clients waiting for me in my room.

"Sign these people up to the firm today. If they have no money, ask them to ask friends for money to pay us directly", he says quickly, walking towards the toilet.

"But if they have no money, they may be entitled to Legal Aid-"

"Don't question me! I am a solicitor of over 30 years, before you were even born", Nemo interrupts me in his usual style. I do not have the energy to argue despite having two espressos and Red Bull coursing through my system.

Later that day a fax does come through. It is from the interviewing officer on behalf of the "Secretary of State for the Home Department".

The letter explains that it is "inconceivable" and "highly shocking" that the events that unfolded earlier that day were allowed to happen, and that Mr. Nguyen has crossed numerous boundaries. However, Mr. Nguyen will be released as a potential victim of torture following a Rule 35 Report, a report that is meant to be prepared by a detention doctor within 48 hours of a detainees arriving and complaining of torture or trafficking, which for some totally not suspicious reason, is rarely produced within 48 hours.

A win for Mr. Nguyen!

Nemo comes to my room after hearing the fax machine. I explain to him the hilarious story of Mr. Nguyen and how he is going to be released soon.

"Very good, Amir! Can we bill his file tonight then?"

October 2019

I hear Nemo stomping up the stairs, laughing and cackling violently at his mobile phone.

"Yes, yes, this boy in the office will see you. I have trained him myself. Come now and bring the money with you."

Like Sherlock Holmes, I am now able to imagine an unfolding scenario with Nemo before it even happens. Unlike Sherlock Holmes, I am unable to avoid them.

"Client coming in 20 minutes. Take her money first. If she does not pay, send her away. Actually don't. Bring her to me", he barks as he barges into my room.

A sour-looking woman in her fifties comes up the stairs. Her eyes darting from corner to corner.

"Where is this Mr. Amir?", she bellows from near the door.

I greet her. Her face reddens and her lips purse. I lead her into my room and try to soften her up.

"Would you like tea or coffee madam? Or maybe water?", I ask, putting on my most friendly voice.

"Where are you from? From… from?", she replies. I ignore the question.

"Are you a solicitor? You don't look like a solicitor to me!"

"I am a trainee solicitor, madam. I am supervised by a solicitor, and Nemo oversees our work too. He is a senior solicitor with over 30 years experience", I explain, regurgitating Nemo's classic sales pitch and punishing line.

"Go on, show me. Start your attendance then, Mr. Amir", she says after eyeing me head to toe.

As I delve into the attendance, reading aloud her paperwork and asking probing questions to get to the bottom of her matter, Ms. Sour-Face starts to shift her chair backwards. I ignore this bizarre antic until she interrupts me by smacking my computer monitor.

"Move this big ugly monitor from the front of your face!" she booms. Her voice resembling that of an angry army major.

"Hang on a second, are you even British? You sound English but you certainly don't look it to me", she quickly follows up.

I now realise that I am being racially profiled, and would say even abused. I end the conversation and ask her to leave my room and sit in reception, where Nemo would see her.

She stands up, gives me a stern stare and walks out. My hands are shaking, but not out of fear, but unbridled anger that I am desperately trying to contain.

I walk to the room Nemo is stationed out. As usual, he was cackling down the phone to some client or potential client, laid back in his seat with one hand stroking his balding head. Before I could speak, he sticks out a finger to signal for me to wait there. I wait and allow him to finish his evidently hilarious conversation with whoever was on the phone.

"Nemo, I believe this potential new client has racially profiled me and is causing me a problem due to this. She has hit my computer monitor, asking me uncomfortable questions about my race-"

"Stop right there. Did you listen to me and take her money?" Nemo interrupts.

"No, I wanted to first understand her situation-"

"You never listen, do you? Send her away. We haven't taken her money anyway so she can't complain", Nemo waves.

"Nemo, I am upset. She has made me feel very uncomfortable", I say, adamant to drive home the pertinent issue of race that the woman appeared to be concerned about.

"Bring her to my office, let me talk to her", Nemo concedes.

I direct Sour-Faced lady to Nemo's room and close the door on them.

I go to Ranveer, who is my direct supervisor and explained the situation. He is shocked and knew immediately that the matter concerned race. We both then hear Nemo and Sour-Faced lady laugh in the other room.

Nemo returns and tells me to go back into my office. He explains to Sour-Face lady that she will have her initial attendance with Ranveer, and another solicitor will have conduct of her matter going forward. Nemo is all grins and teeth, and Sour-Face lady is no longer sour-faced.

Ranveer looks at Nemo confused, but Nemo gives him a stern stare in return. Ranveer begins the attendance. Ranveer explains that her matter will be dealt with by Mr. Johnson in our City office.

"Is he white?", she says unashamedly.

"Yes, he is", Ranveer replies.

Nemo sticks his head in my room and winks at me.

"Don't worry about it. She is just an old woman. We will sign her up on legal aid. We will make money off her", and waltzes off back to his office, and reconvenes a conversation which entails loud belly laughs.

Sour-Face lady leaves the office excitedly. I am now at boiling point, losing my senses and worried I would do something reckless to Nemo. I return to Nemo and confront him.

"Can you not see that the woman was being racist?! You did not have to sign her up. You should have sent her away!" I loudly and sternly tell him. I was sick of being polite and considerate. I can acquiesce to a ridiculous caseload, but I cannot accept racism from clients whilst a director ignores my grievance.

Nemo stands up and shuts the door behind me.

"Don't make a scene in my office! How dare you? I am a solicitor of over 30 years, before you were even born. Also, she said that she didn't say anything racist to you. Do you have any evidence?", he retorts, clearly gearing for an argument.

"Fine, I will contact your brother (Mr. Krabs) and the training principal. They can listen to this issue and deal with it", I reply, and walk away before Nemo goes nuclear.

I email over the attendance note I was making and noted all the comments and actions Sour-Face said and did, and emailed it over to Mr. Krabs and Big B. I ask Mr. Krabs and Big B not to disclose the matter to Nemo as I felt uncomfortable with the way he dismissed the events, and referred them to my supervisor, Ranveer, as a point of contact to get independent information of the events that unfolded.

Nemo begins hovering around my office, muttering under his breath. I close my door, and I can see his silhouette standing outside my room from the window panes of my office door.

The clock strikes 8pm. I receive no response from Big B and Mr. Krabs. Nemo knocks on my door this time. That's a change.

"I am going home now. Don't make this a big issue. I will resolve it. Good-bye. See you tomorrow", he says then walks out.

After a period of ten minutes, Nemo returns to the office as I am packing my things.

"Just to let you know, everything you send to my brother or Big B, I know about! There is no need to make an issue out of something like this. I have your back. I am your director. Actually, I am your uncle! Consider me your father's brother."

"Nemo, I would like to go home. It is late now. Thank you", I respond, unwilling to entertain Nemo's nonsensical antics.

"You do know, Amir, everyone in the City office is working away. By the time I get to the South East England office, the trainee solicitors will be still working. They are such hardworkers. I will personally see to it that they will go far", Nemo's tone changes for the third time in ten minutes.

"Okay, I have no more time for this. Allow me to leave. I am going home", I nip the conversation in the bud and walk out.

The next day, I receive an email from Mr. Krabs. Big B, his wife, naturally did not respond, but I was not expecting a reply from her anyway, seeing as she's been as evasive as Bigfoot.

The email starts with no introduction and goes straight into it.

"You saying to me attendance note you send me last night was drafted at same time? The timing is very interesting… Please explain."

What a bizarre email. Is Mr. Krabs doubting my account of events? And what does he even mean by the "timing is very interesting".

I respond to the email querying exactly that. I get a response, but it is in perfect English, and signed off as Mr. Krabs – director (not Barrister this time), with a detailed signature almost identical to that of Big B.

"Dear Amir,

For the avoidance of any doubt, we are investigating this grave matter. It is just that the attendance note you provided was extremely detailed, and I was trying to understand the chronology of events. I was intrigued to see that you have drafted this very detailed attendance note in an attendance that did not last for more than an hour. Regardless, we as the directors of this firm will look into this. Kind regards, Mr. Krabs – director (with a detailed signature used only by Big B)."

Later that day I check my colleague Mr. Johnson's case list. It has burgeoned by one new client. I check the name of this new client. You guessed it. Ms. Sour-Face.

As I lay there in shock at the complete disregard this firm has for employees' concern, Nemo stormed up the office stairs.

"Why are the blinds down?! Where is the printer paper?! The stairs are dirty! Dirty dirty!", he spouts as he arrives.

He walks straight into my room.

"All emails you send, I am aware of. Also, I have another new client for you today. Sign them up and remember to take money on account first". He then walks to his office, phone in hand, dialing someone, with loud cackling following soon after.

November 2019

Among the desolate, grey landscape of cyclical charging, billing, and signing up of new clients, a green shoot appeared for me in my personal life. My wife was heavily pregnant and the due date was around the corner. Looking back, a lot of the patience I showed was down to the anticipation of this major milestone in my life. Every recent setback, harsh email, rude client, and low pay was all shouldered knowing that any moment now, a pure entity, clean of the machinations of the greedy world, will be born.

My wife and I prepared and furnished our flat for this arrival. We set up a crib right next to our bed, made many visits to Ikea, and baby clothes were folded and stacked in a tiny cupboard prepared for the new arrival.

All I had to do was prepare the workplace, and request some form of paternity leave and cover for my cases.

I spoke to my supervising solicitor, Ranveer, and he said that such things are out of his scope as my supervisor.

I talked to Nemo, who said that such matters should be discussed with someone senior like Mr. Krabs and Big B. Problem is, Mr. Krabs rarely ever visits our office, and Big B remains distanced away from her lowly trainees.

I opt to email them both, explaining that I will need some time off, and that my contract is silent on paternity leave. My email is ignored by both. If the firm had an HR department, I would have approached them, but as with many law firms outside the usual corporate and commercial behemoths, many shockingly do not have one. A director like Mr. Krabs or Big B, or a sycophantic solicitor close to a firm's leadership like Ellga, will deal with such requests as a de facto single-person HR department.

After numerous attempts to call Mr. Krabs and Big B, Mr. Krabs finally picks up.

"Why do you repeat call? I have submission to prepare for big case in Supreme Court", Mr Krabs barks.

I explain to him that my wife is set to give birth soon and I need time off.

"You have not been here long enough to entitle you to paternity leave. Take leave from your annual leave. I have to go now", he interrupts me mid-sentence, in identical fashion to Nemo.

"What about my cases?", I fire back.

"Give them to Mahraja", he replies, and then proceeds to hang up.

I call up Mahraja, and she is crying on the phone. She has been diagnosed with a form of cancer and will be going under the knife soon to extract the tumour. She explains that she is struggling with her own caseload. I do not know what to reply to that. All I could do is apologise for the call.

I try to call back Mr. Krabs. His phone has been switched off.

Nemo stomps up the stairs. Perfect. I will dump my cases on him.

"Hi Nemo, I am going to take a few days off for my paternity leave. Is it possible to babysit my cases? I have brought them up to date and nothing is outstanding at the moment as far as I am aware", I tell him, hoping he will say yes.

"No, I am a director. I have important things to do like oversee this office. Give it to Mahraja", he replies as he tries to make his way to the bathroom.

"But Mahraja is ill. I don't think she has capacity to take on 181 active cases, Nemo", I persist.

"No, she must. Why do we pay her a salary? I will talk to her. I have to go to the bathroom", he waddles away into the bathroom.

Minutes later, I can hear Nemo talk loudly on his mobile in the toilet. I make a mental note never to touch his mobile ever.

Suddenly the toilet door swings open smacking against the doorstop, and Nemo is power-walking to my room.

"Amir, Amir! I have another case for you before you go on your leave. Where are you? There you are! Make sure you sign them up. They are coming now to the office!", Nemo is panting, unable to contain his excitement.

I look down and see that Nemo has left his zip and button undone, and his white underwear is clearly visible. All words remain lodged in my throat. I have prepared for a lot of things in life, but never to tell a money-hungry, middle aged employer that his trousers and fly are undone.

Ranveer, seeing this scene, skips to my office.

"Mr. Nemo! Sir! Your trousers!", he says, with concern on his face.

Nemo looks down, mumbles to himself, and walks away.

As it is a day of wins for me, I decide to take off 10 working days to cover my paternity leave. I hit send. A minute later, I see a notification explaining that my leave has been refused. Mr. Krabs has surprisingly typed a reason:

"Too long"

I apply again, taking off five working days, covering a single week. An hour later, I receive a notification accepting my leave request.

Until today, I am still shocked as to how I did not qualify for at least statutory paternity leave. I was present in the company for more than 26 weeks, was a full-time worker, and was desperately trying to give them notice with no clear channel of communication. Ironically, I was training to be a solicitor and became silver-tongued and persistent in pushing for the rights of my own clients, yet did not know my own rights at my own workplace and the obligations of my employers towards me. The irony of it all still hurts me.

Nevertheless, I believe this is problem that is more common than many would think. I would say the majority of trainees do not want to sabotage or anger their superiors, and are willing to swallow grievance after grievance to get through the training contract unscathed, and to keep alive their chances of a permanent NQ (newly qualified) role after qualification. Mentioning this, training contract providers in my opinion are fully aware of this imbalance of bargaining power and experience. They would extract as much time and labour from you as possible, with an active disregard for your anemic salary, your physical and mental health (characters like Mahraja exist in almost every firm I have been to), and most importantly your statutory rights. They will almost always try to get away with it, feigning ignorance of the personal development in your life.

> *Mental health? What mental health? Fatherhood? You did not tell us. Your leave entitlement? Refer to your contract. But my contract doesn't state…? Contact X or Y – they will assist you, as I cannot help. Cancer? What?*

Unfortunately and unsurprisingly, most trainees will avoid a clash with their employers, and sadly opt to 'firm' the abuse to get by. A trainee cannot afford to iron or hash out a perfectly drafted and bilaterally agreed contract with the backing of an entourage of legal counsel prior to signing on for a training contract. The firm, on signs of trepidation from you, will pull the contract and offer it to someone else. Thousands of law graduates will jump at the opportunity to take your place. The argument to 'negotiate your contract' is true for other spheres of employment, but a trainee solicitor, usually naïve, eager and desperate, will sign anything to get their foot through the door and on the road to qualification. If they don't snatch at the opportunity, they will remain bitter and confused on the by-line, wondering how others got in.

10. Merry Christmas, 2019

After I became a father to a brand new baby, I returned to work with a spring in my step, ready to take on whatever case Jobsons were going to throw at me. Attempting to change nappies soiled by brightly-coloured liquid poos (which I then delegated to my wife permanently like a team player) surely prepared me for the worst.

I returned to the office. 63 voicemails? Nice. 112 missed calls? Very nice. Let me trigger a cardiac arrest by opening up my email inbox. 124 emails? Did I leave the auto-reply confirming my absence or are they blind?

The trainee in my office was soon to qualify around this time, and he was desperately awaiting an update in relation to a job offer. Mr. Krabs was startlingly at the office and intended to negotiate with this trainee.

Mr. Krabs entered the trainee's room and cut straight to the chase, leaving the door wide open for the indulgence of the rest of us.

"How much you want for new solicitor salary?"

"I was looking at the Law Society website, and there is an average solicitor's salary mentioned, something along the lines of 36,000GBP"

"Haha, no, no, no. We are a high street firm, not US corporate firm. You are funny. That is not us. I will offer you 27000GBP. Yes or no?"

"Sorry, that is starting too low, Mr. Krabs… I would think-"

"Final offer. I will wait outside. If not, then sorry you will have to look elsewhere. Good luck", Mr. Krabs finished and walked out.

Mr. Krabs walks into my room.

"How is the baby? Good? Your billing, I looked at it. Only two times your salary. This is worst one in the firm. Andy in South East England office outperforming you. You have no excuse"

"I just came back from lea-"

"No more excuses. Remember, you are lucky to be trainee. Tough market. Many people want your position", Mr. Krabs uttered and walked out, playing with the key fob to his latest BMW i8.

Five minutes later, Mr. Krabs came back to say good bye. That's nice of him.

"Hi Amir, I am leaving now. Take care. Also, trainee next door is leaving. So, you will take his cases", he said smiling this time.

"But Mr. Krabs, I have no capacity whatsoever, I have 15 cases in the Upper Tribunal and-"

"Don't talk over me! Dig deep. You are trainee, I worked 18 hours as trainee 30 years ago!", his smile vanished, replaced with a red-eyed deep stare, before proceeding to slam my door shut.

Merry Christmas, Amir.

Email comes in from Big B at that moment.

"Dear colleagues,

As you are aware, we are extremely busy over the Christmas and New Years. As such, you are all expected to share responsibilities and fully cover the Christmas period. All offices will remain open other than on the usual bank holidays."

And a happy new year, Amir.

27 December 2019

Okay, let me break the UK asylum process to you in simple terms to bring you a little into the work I was dealing with at the time. It begins with a story. The asylum-seeker takes that story and must then claim asylum at the port or at the Home Office's main office in Croydon. They must explain their story and reasons as to why they cannot go back to their country of origin in two interviews, a screening interview and a substantive interview. A screening interview lasts about ten minutes but involves a wait time in the Home Office's office of up to six hours where you cannot use your phone, you are watched via CCTV, and cannot leave the building unless in an emergency. Whilst a substantive interview lasts for as long as it takes, sometimes broken down over two days if the asylum-seeker's story is particularly detailed. Over such interviews, the Home Office 'interviewing' officer fleshes out the full story and decides whether such a person deserves to be recognised and protected under the Refugee Convention, or to be refused. A decision is served on the Applicant via a 'detailed' letter (usually a copy and paste of numerous others).

After some time, it has become achingly obvious that most of the Jobson asylum-seeking clients all had the exact same fear of the same people from the same country. After reading through hundreds of their witness statements and bundles of evidence, they were, again, almost identical, with at times just the dates and names changed.

I popped my head into Ranveer's office. He had his headphones in and Beethoven's fifth Symphony was blaring beyond the noise-cancellation abilities.

"Do these claims ever get accepted? They are ridiculously similar. Surely they are flagged up for some sort of suspicion", I said, trying to hide the panic in my voice thinking about any potential audit of my files by the Legal Aid Agency, or worse, the SRA.

"I haven't seen a single one being refused or dismissed completely. If the Home Office do not accept, the courts end up allowing their claims on appeal. Here, see the drawer where their refugee residence permits are", Ranveer said.

He pulled open a drawer under his desk and it was chockfull of Biometric Residence Permits (the card now given to evidence their lawful residence instead of a vignette or stamp in their passports) of these clients with identical surnames and claims.

My mind goes back to my old client Mr. Farah. Desperately trying to argue his claim to stay in a country that he has known since childhood yet faced the very real threat of forced removal from the country, having to attend court hearing after hearing to resist deportation.

When migrants face an increasingly complex myriad of red tape and bureaucracy to regularise their stay in the UK, the successful ones are the ones that usually deploy the most simplistic method through the easiest route to residency – a bit of an immigration Occam's razor.

Critics of migration would back the blanket withdrawal from the Refugee Convention. For those unaware, the Refugee Convention 1951 bestows asylum-seekers the right to claim asylum, and obligates signatory States like the UK to consider them. Yet withdrawing from this international agreement attacks the symptoms of an imagined problem more than anything else. Withdraw from the Refugee Convention and the identically-named clients will figure out an alternative route through the Immigration Rules, such as the spouse route, or the long residence route, or the student route. I saw it in practice time and again. Say we take it one step further, withdraw from the Refugee Convention, and also close the vast majority of routes to residence currently available under the Immigration Rules. In such an instance, who would really want to come to the UK? Can you seriously bank on Britain's pull to attract the cream of the crop of the intellectual world; the scientists, the engineers and doctors? Do you honestly believe they would repeatedly choose the UK over let us say the countries still in the European Union, such as Germany and France? In addition, whilst the UK has now withdrawn from the EU, competition has deepened further as we rub shoulders with our rivals on the other side of the pond – the USA and Canada, as well as across the pacific in Australia and New Zealand. Can you reasonably argue that the hypothetical foreign scientist would choose the UK over the US or Australia, or an EU country that allows her free movement in the bloc?

Say this scientist does end up choosing the UK, she has to then pay two quite substantial fees immediately, with no guarantee of acceptance: the Home Office fee (which varies depending on visa type but range from a few hundreds to a few thousands), and the Immigration Health Surcharge (IHS) which has gone up to 624GBP per year.

It is always funny, and by funny, I mean aneurysm-inducing fury, hearing how immigrants are exhausting our National Health Service. Yet immigrants are our biggest sponsors of the service, with millions upon millions pumped into it directly through their Immigration Health Surcharge payments.

Say the foreign scientist wants to bring over her husband; she will have to pay his Home Office fee and the IHS covering his time in the UK. She then decides to bring over her children too since she cannot leave them alone abroad with her ageing parents. Again, the same story applies, and again the Home Office and IHS fees are to be paid for each of her children. By the time this scientist gets permanent residence, known as Indefinite Leave to Remain after five years, she would have spent north of 8000GBP. If she ends up loving the UK and wishes to naturalise, we're talking about more money paid to the Secretary of State for the Home Department, along with a Life in the UK Test asking you questions about an English King's favourite cereal and time he slept (this part I made up). What about her now integrated children? They can be naturalised but their application costs 1012GBP (at time of writing). A four-figure sum for a child's application. A figure higher of the same application type in almost any developed country in the world.

The Secretary of State for the Home Department has vilified immigrants yet lines her pockets with their money, whilst making a fist and shaking her head to appease populist sentiments which have seeped in various parts of the nation. The Leader of Opposition is not any better, barely making a squeak out of this all.

Let us take the hypothetical scenario to its extreme. Let us say we close up shop, from the asylum to all other immigration routes. The UK will no longer have Filipino nurses that keep the entire NHS ticking, the Vietnamese and Chinese restaurants that help feed and strengthen the local economies of various regions of the UK, the African care home staff that take care of our ageing population, the Australian teachers that bolster the fatigued education system, and the Indian technicians that keep the IT infrastructure running. The ones we do currently have, do you really think they would want to stay any longer? A press that has vilified them. A government that has had a hand in their pocket from the moment they arrived, and frowns when they bring over their family members.

Whilst we are at it, let us deport Mr. Farah back to Somalia. I am sure his mental health issues will certainly not be exploited by pervasive terrorist groups in the region, from Al-Shabab to

Alqaeda. Oh and it was definitely Somalia where he picked up his criminal habits, and not the streets of Harlesden in the UK, right?

The argument is of course one of nuance, which I am not downplaying. Resources are finite and arguments against an open border are also persuasive and lengthy. As with most things in life, the answer likely lies somewhere between the two extremes and it is a balance, a sane, pragmatic and thoughtful UK government of the future that will have to find the answer. Rant over.

11. Contagion

February 2020

I met up with one of my close friends who I have not seen for quite some time. I was caught up in the world of law, and he was caught up trying to impress his corporate overlords in the City.

We sat down for dinner at a Far Asian restaurant in Queensway, off Hyde Park.

I would use this friend as a stress ball, pleading the injustices that have befallen on oneself. He was and still is a fantastic ear, and I would thoroughly recommend all those working in an intense field to befriend someone like that.

I slurp my soup and this friend is particularly quiet. He is a natural germaphobe and there has been a topic that he has not stopped talking about since November last year.

"What is it called again? What 19? Where?" I am trying to make sense of his ramblings with every swallow.

"Listen Amir, there is a virus that has been discovered in Wuhan which has now spread throughout the world. The World Health

Organisation have been warning us all! Read here!", he points at small texts on a screenshot on his phone.

I nod profusely.

I return to work the next day, bloated and bursting at the seams with last night's food. I make a mental note to update my trouser wardrobe. Started at 28inches, now at 32inches, and it feels as tight as ever.

I walk in to the office and Ranveer is walking up and down the corridor, in his classic panic mode.

"What is it Ranveer? Also, good morning", I tell him to cheer him up.

"My brother works as a doctor in the front line! He has a cough! I think he has this novel COVID-19 virus!", Ranveer is sweating, beads forming on his receding hairline.

I ignore him and walk to my room to attend to the 14 missed calls I had over night, and the angry email from Big B lambasting me for not replying to all 14 missed calls, that had to be rerouted to the reception and caused a "wasting of resources".

However, Ranveer has not stopped. He has called Mr. Krabs and they are talking to each other over loudspeaker.

"Mr. Krabs, there is a virus. I have read that it is worse than the Spanish Flu. Listen to me, we have to not come in to the office!", Ranveer screeched.

In hindsight, maybe Ranveer should have been the health secretary ahead of Matt Hancock. He was ahead of the curve before the Conservative government knew what social distancing was.

"No need to panic, Ranveer. It is like influenza, ha ha. Don't you have work? I have looked at your timesheet and it is low for today". Mr. Krabs swatted away all of Ranveer's concerns before hanging up.

Nemo did not attend the office that day or the day after. Odd.

23 March 2020

The UK entered a full lockdown following the spread of COVID-19. Boris Johnson appeared on television urging people to work from home. Yet, here we were. All in the office on a day when the busy streets of North West London finally quietened down to a deafening silence.

We all collectively emailed Mr. Krabs, Big B, Mr. Jobson (no one even knows if he was still alive), and Nemo.

Finally, after numerous emails and calls, Big B sent out a firmwide email.

"Dear colleagues,

For the avoidance of doubt, you are expected to continue to work from the office. If you have any medical conditions or living with vulnerable people at home, please explain this to us no later than the end of day today, and we will decide whether to allow you to work from home."

I quickly emailed back explaining that I visit my elderly parents who will fall in the vulnerable group. Big B did respond to me. She graced me with a reply. Praise be.

"Dear Amir,

As you explained clearly in your email, you "visit" your parents. As such, you do not live with them. For the avoidance of doubt, I make clear to you Amir, that you are expected to work in the office. Also, please leave the doors open and lights on throughout the day to allow clients to walk in unhindered. I have received reports from Nemo that you shut the front door. I would like to remind you that you are working out of a high-street branch of our business, and we are a business."

I look out of the window. Not a single soul walking the street. Which clients? What business?

I pack the office laptop and drive home. A national lockdown and I am in the office, suited and booted, doors wide open and lights on, for whom exactly? The appeasement of maniacs, I scream to myself.

Ranveer calls me.

"Come back to the office, Amir! You did not get permission from Mr. Krabs or Big B! You will get us all in trouble!"

I reject his calls. He calls me from Whatsapp. I block him on that.

I begin work from the office laptop in the comfort of my living room. Surprisingly, I log the same amount of billable time that day, and following days, than the days I was working from the office.

Thankfully, it transpires that a revolt has broken out in the other offices aswell, where the trainees have also refused to come in. The management's hands were now forced. They acquiesce, but it did not stop them sending a vicious email, which reads:

"Dear trainees,

We have looked after your interests in the midst of a lockdown, ahead of the immediate well-being of the firm. We have continued to pay salaries on time, and have, as of yet, not made anyone redundant – though this might change at any time.

For the avoidance of doubt, you are all now expected to bill 8 hours a day instead of your usual 6. This is because you will have no distractions, and do not need to commute to work. No time wasted and very little admin on your ends. We will review the billing of each trainee at the end of each day. Those who do not provide a sufficient reason for not meeting their billable times will be let go – as per your contracts.

Kind regards,

Management"

The "avoidance of doubt" made it abundantly clear who drafted that email. Hilariously, the country was at a standstill, and prospective clients were not exactly banging on firm doors at this minute. No one really wanted to move houses so the conveyancing solicitors largely had to try to deal with their current caseload. Air and seaports shut, so immigration largely ground to a halt, and non-criminal detainees were being released from all detention centres. So business at Jobsons was not exactly booming.

Unsurprisingly, all offices were downsized within the space of two months. The North West office was shaved down to just me and Ranveer. The family solicitor was made redundant, the paralegal that visited was told her time was up, and we were told that we now had to cover all incoming calls and emails to that particular office. Moreover, Ranveer and I were to rotate in coming in and attending to all affairs of the office.

The South East office had various trainees put on furlough leave, and were told point blank that the batch that is to qualify the soonest will not be offered any newly qualified roles.

The reception team in the South East were let go, and the single admin was made to do reception work, admin work, and the post.

The firm staff were essentially culled.

Mr. Krabs sent out an email to all trainees accidentally, when it was intended for the South East office only.

"Hello, Mr. Krabs Barrister here. You will all be furlaughed. After, you will be have to find new jobs.

Good luck.

Mr. Krabs Barrister"

Yes, the email was that blunt, and yes, he called the furlough scheme "furlaugh". I still laugh about that.

12. Socially Distancing from Sanity

The coming months went by surprisingly quickly. I would attend one day, Ranveer the day after, and so on. I would come in, open the shutters, open the door wide open as Nemo likes it, turn on all the lights, including the toilet lights as directed by Nemo, and begin work, alone in an office.

The eerie silence allowed me to enter a sort of Zen where I put my head down and plough out the hours.

The days I work from home were starting to become a bit of a challenge. My child was waking my wife in all sorts of weird and wonderful hours of the night.

I took the executive decision to set-up a blow-up bed in the living room that became my permanent abode. I wake, roll off the bed, turn on the laptop, and get to work.

On one of the days that I worked from home, I missed my 8 hours of billable work. By 7pm, I get an email from Big B.

"You did not hit your billable hours for today. Please explain immediately. Failure to provide a sufficient excuse can result in the termination of your training contract."

I would respond with the following:

"Dear Big B,

I booked a half-day annual leave. Mr. Krabs and Big B both approved it on the leave portal. See screenshot attached."

She replies immediately.

"Dear Amir, I do not appreciate this snarky reply. But for the avoidance of doubt, you are not to work during your annual leave if you have booked it."

"Dear Big B, thank you for your reminder. Noted for the future."

Whatever rocks your boat, Big B. Just don't cause an issue with the signing off of my training contract which is due in a few months.

The following day I attend the office, as it was my turn to sit there alone for hours on end. I arrive half an hour early as the buses now have a clear and uninterrupted route, with no open schools.

Someone is already there. I walk up slowly and all the lights are on and there is a scraping sound coming from within. I creep and I hear loud groans, followed by a large bang.

"Hello?", I bellow. I am paid excessively little to also be a bodyguard for this firm.

Finally, the figure behind the noise appears. It is Nemo. He is setting up a table for himself in one of the rooms.

"Hi Amir. I will be here early every day permanently from now on. This office is making us very little money. You and Ranveer are slacking. South East office is performing better than you both. Also, there will be a meeting with Mr. Krabs every morning via Microsoft Teams. Everyone is to tell him what work they will be doing at exactly 8:30am. Now come and help me set up my new table."

Making very little money, you say? Yes, new clients dried up, but old clients were continuing to pay us. My actual billing, thankfully, was not faltering. As for Ranveer, he was carrying out judicial review challenges that have largely been a success, allowing him to recoup pay for the firm at an 'inter partes' rate, which essentially means take whatever your billing for that file and multiply it by three. Most of his judicial review files had hundreds of hours of work. A single file had 15,000GBP worth of 'profit costs' (money charged for each action he took on the file). Meaning on that single file, he will bank for the firm 45,000GBP.

It became sickeningly clear to me that the "management" of Mr. Krabs, Big B, and his brother, Nemo, only cared about the bottom line: money. Nepotism and narcissism was running rife and they would will lie, lie and lie some more to try to squeeze out a little more money from us. They would cull teams, and end trainees' dreams if it interfered in any way with their money. As long as they rake in money, then all is fair. Even if that involves lying, point blank about the offices performances, trainee billing, or anything else for that matter. We were nothing but golden geese laying golden eggs, and they will come and collect at the end of every month. No training or clear rights for us, and no obligations on them.

My health began to deteriorate. A lockdown on top and it was I on the ropes. The first alarm bell that rang was an abundance of hair loss. Then frequent headaches which felt like the back of my eyes were about to burst from pressure.

I ignored the first alarm bells. Ibuprofen here and there cycled with paracetamol would sort it out. It did not.

The second alarm bells I could not ignore. I would stand and have a dizzying sensation. Stabbing back pains would begin around where I would imagine the kidneys are.

I would wake up and see that I have wet myself, followed by difficulties going back to sleep.

I went to the GP and they took a series of blood works. The results came back confusing. Low iron, low Vitamin D, low Vitamins B6 and B12. As well as an elevated blood pressure, floating around 140/90. I was only in my late twenties. If I get COVID-19, would I get a few days off work though? Oh yes, and morbid thoughts were another alarm bell.

I was asked for a stool sample and more blood was taken.

The following months, Nemo travelled early every day to the office, but before that, starting his journey in the South East office, no doubt pestering some other sorry trainee. The roundtrip alone is surely over four hours for him, but despite his age, his bursting beer belly, and his horrifically simple diet of biscuits and tea, he would continue to do it.

With each visit, he would pick up random sods off the streets needing help with their immigration matters, telling them we can resolve their matters once and for all with a simple one-off fee paid to him.

I would flag up various issues with these random cases, and explain as politely as possible, that the current crop of evidence these new clients are providing suggests they will not be able to stay in the UK as "highly skilled workers", working in, checks notes, entrepreneurs in door-to-door sales. Nemo would pull me aside, scream and point angrily at me, and then command me to take their money. I go back in, quote whatever Nemo mentions, get given money in cash, whereby it is snatched out of my hands by Nemo who walks to the bank to deposit it. If I have to put my finger on when my blood pressure really spikes, it is when Nemo is involved.

Nemo's ingenuity knew no bounds. He began looking through my case list, eyeing up those on legal aid. He would then call them up and break down tasks that I am set to do, but with a twist.

He would say a specific action, like requesting their file from another firm or approaching their GP for their medical records is "not covered by legal aid", and they would have to pay us privately for these actions. A number would be plucked out of thin air, and they would, shockingly, pay him time and again. Which meant more occasions of Nemo snatching cash out of my hands to go down to the bank to deposit.

This was surely crossing some sort of ethical line. I finally had the courage to question him about this. I explained that legal aid clients are on legal aid for a reason. He knew exactly where the conversation was going. He cut me off, explaining, "we are a business, we have to make money. Also, I have spoken to Mr. Krabs and Big B. They said it is fine".

The next day during my now daily Microsoft Teams meeting with Mr. Krabs, he made sure to single me out.

"Amir, I heard you are causing problem in North West. We are a business and very legal. I have been barrister for more than 30 years, before you were born. Remember, you are a trainee and have billing to make. You need more cases because you are not really busy."

Looks like Nemo's speech about his 30 years' experience has a source. Later that day, 16 new cases were allocated to me. I officially crossed the 200 active cases mark, and have missed five court deadlines already. Thankfully, they accepted my COVID-19 excuses about business challenges and need for extensions of time for all. I no longer worked to bolster or improve individual appeal matters. Professional third party evidence like psychiatric reports, scarring reports, independent social workers reports to support my clients' cases were no longer my priority, as to attempt to obtain funding will take so much time that by the time the Legal Aid Agency confirms funding, Nemo and Mr. Krabs would have forced me to take an additional 16 new cases. My conscience hurt knowing that I was no longer representing my clients to the very highest standards, but I was being drowned in cases and was just thinking about getting to the shoreline.

13. Finish Line

I finally reached the final month of my training contract in February 2021. One month exactly, and I will be signed off by Big B (the training principal that provided me with precisely naught training), and admitted to the Solicitors Roll. I had no intention of staying on even if they put the sun in my right hand and moon in my left. This was largely understood by Nemo, who I clashed with again and again, yet he kept on piling the cases with the full backing of Mr. Krabs.

I looked at myself in the mirror and saw new creases on my forehead. The white of my eyes were no longer white, rather a hue of yellow, with angry looking arteries swarming through them. My wrists clicked and my knees grinded. My back hunched, and neck jutted forward.

I sit down in the local park, eating a ploughman, which formed the staple of my diet, and mentally assessed my own performance over the two years.

I had definitely learnt a lot thanks to an insane and varied caseload.

Public law, essentially the challenge of public authorities like the Home Office and Police, was something that I became adept at.

Immigration from private as well as business, to legally aided, I knew like the back of my own hands.

I assisted the litigation solicitor here and there with TOLATA claims, which are disputes involving people who once lived in the same property, fighting over the rights to it, as well as litigating our own clients for non-payment on behalf of Big B, I mean the firm.

All in all, I was happy I managed to train myself and put myself in situations where I gained relevant experience in three distinct areas of law (no longer a necessity according to the SRA rules), in spite of the management's attempt to bog me down with flimsy but private-paying immigration applications.

I mentally gave myself a pat on the back, chomped on my ploughmans, and started scrolling through Instagram.

Whilst on Instagram, I repeatedly see the posts of a particular lawyer, who dabbles in public speaking and has organisations dedicated to 'assisting' BME wannabe lawyers. I have observed her feed on social media from afar, and she has made it her market to fill out venues, and obtain various government-related funds in her seemingly selfless quest to assist law graduates from poorer backgrounds.

Despite all the noise, fancy pictures of herself in a wig posing outside the Royal Courts of Justice, very little substance can be made out from her posts.

I repeatedly see images of her looking judicial, yet her posts where she dishes out advice were stale nonsense, that enlarged her profile more than provide any particular takeaways for young graduates.

To give an example, she refers to all solicitors and barristers as "lawyers", despite there being a major difference (essentially showing she caters to a dumbed down audience), and telling graduates to "work hard and cold call day and night" big corporate firms, to "put yourself out there and be recognised". There are too many layers of nonsense to unpack here. Firstly, big corporate law firms have specific windows for trainees to join, that involves various tests, online applications, and assessment centres. No amount of cold calling will make them bend their very fixed process to let your special person in.

Secondly, she repeatedly uploads a picture of herself in a wig and gown. She is a criminal barrister herself, so I am confused as to how she is confident in advising graduates that are not pursuing the type of "lawyer" she is in the first place. Criminal law at the Bar is entirely different from corporate and commercial law in a Magic Circle firm!

To compound matters, and maybe this is envy which I would freely admit, she has essentially fell on good times and is not afraid to show her large palatial home, expensive range of wines in her wine cellar, and flashy watches and red-heeled shoes. She always leaves an 'inspirational' quote or piece of advice for the young wannabe lawyers which is usually a rehash of "chase your dream", or to "dress smart or the firm won't hire your dumb ass". Again, way too much to unpack. One of the most senior solicitors I met ran around the offices I worked in barefoot with a Simpsons tie spun in a knot, and a scruffy Zizec-style beard. Yet, was driving the latest Porsche, and was a legal genius. This idea that you have to dress like Harvey Specter from Suits is fiction and will always be.

Secondly, numerous criminal barristers, God bless them, have largely fallen on tough times. A recent BBC article illustrates the plight some of them go through, travelling from court to court all over the country, paid less than minimum wage (for the hours they put in), and the costs and fees that they have to keep to ensure the feed comes in. A side-by-side comparison with a worker at a fast-food chain in many instances is earning more than a criminal barrister. Some criminal barristers are making 5.80GBP an hour, and earning less than 16,000GBP a year. Don't believe me? Look it up.

Yet, Mrs. Instagram Lawyer will have you believe that once you are 'in', you will immediately fall into the glitz and glamour of the Legal Broadway. She is silent on the Bar Professional Training Course fees, which have now risen 18,735GBP in certain London universities, the long nights of studying, the extreme difficulties (yes, barristers are outnumbered 8 to 1 by solicitors) in getting pupillage (the training contract for barristers), and the likelihood that pay would be meagre for years if not decades. Unless you hit the big time defending the UK version of OJ Simpson, you will start smaller than small, and grow to medium at best. That can similarly be said to trainee solicitors, who will have to walk on broken glass, jump through burning hoops, and sweat their blood in bodyweight, before being picked among a small, select few to join a well-paying firm, usually a legal 500 corporate and commercial outfit, or a US firm. And with good pay comes ridiculously unsocial hours. A friend, who did train at one particular firm of such an ilk, remained in the office for four consecutive days to help his supervisor finalise a deal. To cut a long story short, he developed symptoms akin to Post-traumatic Stress Disorder, and resigned soon after his training contract came to an end. He spends his time now walking in parks and rambling on podcasts.

Young readers, do not let online legal charlatans trick you into a fictitious reality of the legal field. It is not the world of witty put-downs in court, or suited and booted strides in sky-high glass buildings, or selfies outside the Royal Court of Justice. I can say that without malice and with love and affection in hope that if you do choose the legal route, it is a calculated and rational one. There are both financial and emotional consequences to your decision. Look to a solicitor or barrister in the field you're interested in and has successfully walked the long walk. Get guidance from them, not social media sharks looking to bang a buck out of futile and vacuous 'training seminars' and 'meet-ups'. You will only walk away with free pens and a bag of cheap goodies. If some lawyers you see online are living like Pablo Escobar, they probably have dealings like Pablo Escobar.

14. The Shock

February 2021

I drag myself into the office on the first day of my final month of my training contract. Before I walk into my room, I give myself a quick pep talk, telling myself that I am almost there. The finish line is indeed in sight. All I need to do is to walk it home.

I login to my PC and boot up my Outlook. Tens of emails over the weekend populate the inbox.

"Urgent! Help me brother!", one screeches. "Worst firm in the world", another opines. "Thank you so much for your help! My family are all here now", a third reads.

But one caught my attention immediately. It was from Big B, and titled "Your Training Contract". My stomach churned. Is this the confirmation of the successful sign off of my training records?

"Dear Amir,

Due to the difficult times on our business due to COVID-19, we have taken the difficult decision to extend your training contract for an additional six months – pending a further review at the end of the decision. We may decide to extend this further.

Moreover, we are aware that you have completed seats in Immigration Law and Human Rights (Private, Business, and Legal Aid) and Public Law. However, your time with our litigation solicitor was insufficient to be counted as a seat.

As you started your training contract before November 2019, the applicable requirements are under the SRA Training Regulations 2014. As such, you are required to complete three distinct seats (rather than simply contentious and non-contentious work). For the avoidance of doubt, you have only completed two – litigation is not counted as sufficient in our opinion.

As such, you will complete a third seat in our Employment department. I will send you notes, and the former employment trainee, who has now successfully qualified, will be passing on his cases to you. Bear in mind that you will also retain your current immigration and public law cases, which we expect you to continue work on.

Kind regards

Signed: Management"

A ringing began in my ear as soon as I started reading, and by the end of the email, I began hearing my heart beat and swooshing of blood in my vessels. I do not know what stage of a psychiatric crisis I was entering, but I was glued to my seat losing my composure to breathe properly.

At that moment, some inner mental strength galvanised to the surface and took control. My brain began compartmentalising and analysing the issues, and I was beginning to think about how to turn around this situation. I will not lose to these charlatans, nor would the last two years go in vain. It was clear that this was a ploy to retain my services to further bulk up their bank accounts whilst paying me peanuts for a salary. I am no longer your golden goose!

I first call up the other trainee in the South East office that I was sure was going to qualify with me. She picks up yet she is not in the office. She has received a similar email but was altered to state that she will be covering the works in the crime department. I ask what her plan to resist is. She has none. She has already had a breakdown and was away on leave for two more weeks.

Well, that's no help.

I call up the SRA hotline and get put through to an operator. I explain my conundrum, holding back tears of anger and anguish. The telephone operator explains that the SRA do have power to sign off a trainee solicitor's training, and admit him/her into the roll. But I will need to evidence this in the form of training records, the Legal Practice Certificate, and a clean DBS. I have all of these.

I prepare the necessary documents into a bundle and dispatch to the relevant SRA email.

I then prepare a scathing email in reply to "management", aka Big B, but make sure that it does not cross professional boundaries.

"Dear Big B,

Thank you for your email.

You have evidently not reviewed my training records which I have provided you. As you can see, I have completed works in immigration law, public law, and human rights. As such, even if you do not believe I have completed a sufficient seat in civil and criminal litigation, human rights is a seat in and of itself.

You have taken my time and hard work in the firm lightly. I do not agree to your terms of extension.

Kind regards,

Amir"

A response comes in fresh and hot within minutes.

"Dear Amir,

I do not appreciate the tone of your email. Further, provide me with proof that human rights is a separate seat.

If you do not agree to an extension, we will terminate your contract and you can find another firm to complete your training and to sign you off.

Big B"

I lob one back. Do not fall on your sword in the face of a retreating enemy. Probably Sun Tzu. If not, then I take full credit for it.

"Dear Big B,

Please see a training manual drafted by the SRA clearly noting 'human rights' as an individual seat. Moreover, you state all of this, yet signed off the training of the previous trainee in the North West office who completed human rights as an independent seat, and had an identical training cycle.

Kind regards,

Amir"

"Dear Amir,

For the avoidance of doubt, I am the training principal and you do not know the details of the training I personally provided to the former trainee.

Big B"

If I ever assume total power, the phrase "for the avoidance of doubt" will be wiped clean off the face of the Earth.

"Dear Big B,

For the avoidance of doubt, I have notified the SRA about your intent to extend the training contract with no concrete end date based on COVID-19 and the veracity of human rights being considered a separate seat.

Kind regards,

Amir"

"Dear Amir,

I will look into your query and get back to you soon. Do not do anything rash.

Kind regards,

Big B"

Bull's eye. I caught her in a compromised position. I believed she will make a U-turn. I have to believe it.

A few days pass and no response from either the SRA or Big B. I attempt to call Big B and she does not pick up. She has rarely picked up any of my calls, so I wasn't particularly shocked, but was certainly in a state of heightened anxiety with each passing day. I call her secretary, and she whispers down the phone to me, "Amir, she knows you're calling but is telling me not to pick up. But you didn't hear it from me, alright?"

In the interim, I continued to work on my cases to distract my mind.

26 February 2021

On the final day of my fixed term training contract, I still had no update and Big B's minion emails me explaining that my time at the firm is coming to an end by end of day today, and a P45 will be posted to me. I query if my training contract will be signed off. She says that that is a decision solely for Big B to decide.

I ring out ten missed calls to her number.

As the clock strikes six, an email comes in from the SRA.

"Your organisation has approved your period of recognised training.

Sign in to complete your application and apply for admission."

Years of training, a rollercoaster of emotions, thousands of clients, and it is finally done. My eyes watered and my legs stopped shaking. I stood up and just soaked in the moment.

Amir, you have done it, I told myself repeatedly. Amir, you have done it. Amir, you have done it.

I called my wife and the relief, shock and happiness overwhelmed the feelings of anxiety, depression and melancholy.

I packed my bags, cleared my desk, and prepared to leave this place permanently. Never again will I let any person dangle a carrot in front of me. My solicitor aspiration ticked off.

I closed the lights and head for the door. At the door, Nemo is awaiting, with a beaming smile, showing all rows of his crooked, cigarette-stained teeth.

"Well done, Amir! You are one of the best trainees, sorry I mean solicitor, I have seen in over 30 years. How about you stay here permanently as a newly qualified solicitor? Mr. Krabs says he will offer you 25,000GBP? What do you say? Eh, buddy?"

I shake my head and head for the exit.

Nemo bellows at me like a possessed auctioneer, "what about 26,000GBP? Let's shake on 27,000GBP!"

I walk out beyond the gates and do not look back. With each step, I feel a weight fall off my shoulders. By the time I get home, I am floating. I open the door and celebrate with my family, my true priority – my wife and young child.

Priorities readjusted.

A new start away from this journey, and with that new hope.

Printed in Dunstable, United Kingdom